AMAZING Beauty

Su Proctor

WESTBOW
PRESS
A DIVISION OF THOMAS NELSON
& ZONDERVAN

Copyright © 2014 Su Proctor.

All rights reserved. No part of this book may be used or reproduced by any means, graphic, electronic, or mechanical, including photocopying, recording, taping or by any information storage retrieval system without the written permission of the publisher except in the case of brief quotations embodied in critical articles and reviews.

WestBow Press books may be ordered through booksellers or by contacting:

WestBow Press
A Division of Thomas Nelson & Zondervan
1663 Liberty Drive
Bloomington, IN 47403
www.westbowpress.com
1 (866) 928-1240

Because of the dynamic nature of the Internet, any web addresses or links contained in this book may have changed since publication and may no longer be valid. The views expressed in this work are solely those of the author and do not necessarily reflect the views of the publisher, and the publisher hereby disclaims any responsibility for them.

Any people depicted in stock imagery provided by Thinkstock are models, and such images are being used for illustrative purposes only. Certain stock imagery © Thinkstock.

ISBN: 978-1-4908-4944-7 (sc)
ISBN: 978-1-4908-4946-1 (e)

Library of Congress Control Number: 2014915329

Printed in the United States of America.

WestBow Press rev. date: 9/22/2014

Amazing Beauty is dedicated to all women and couples who have ever experienced difficulty with having a baby. Whether it's infertility or being unable to carry a pregnancy to full term, please know that you are not alone.

Not Alone

*So far what I have sewn
Life that I have known*

*I am missing
There has to be more*

*Jesus, even after all I bore
is there something better in store?*

"Yes, My yoke is easy and burden light"

*Lord, I let go
No more living in the night
I will love you with all my heart and might*

*I have a friend,
Let me introduce Jesus*

*He is with us and for us
providing everything joyous*

*me and He
Now and into eternity we will be*

Chapter 1

It's Valentine's Day, February 2014, and I am home alone. Joe, my husband, is away on a men's retreat with our church. He left yesterday and will be back tomorrow afternoon. Since I have this time to myself, I read over a few of my favorite verses and prayed. There's nothing on television, even though we have every channel imaginable, and while I have this time to myself to do anything I want, I am led to write my story.

How do I begin sharing the most painful part of my life so far? Other than a handful of people, not too many know what happened to us, and those who do know some of our story lack the details. Even our families do not know the complete extent of the experiences. As a matter of fact, I kept a lot of my personal insecurities, hurt, and embarrassment from my husband, even. I was an utter mess, and while I was living in inner torment, the Lord was with me the entire time, waiting for me realize that healing begins with me acknowledging I want to be better.

I am sharing my story for several reasons: first and foremost, to acclaim the goodness of my God, to whom I have access in my Lord and Savior, Jesus Christ. Second, I have been putting this off and putting this off for over a year now. The Holy Spirit has been pressing on me to write this, and I have been stubbornly ignoring that guidance and am finally listening (my husband has also been dropping comments over the past year to write a book, but let's give all the credit to the Holy Spirit). Another important reason for me to relive all this is in hopes that, by sharing my story and pointing them to the chief healer, Jesus Christ, others will heal or begin the healing process.

There are so many stories inside of this story, but one specific aspect is the main focus of this crazy tale. You see, over the past five years I have experienced four miscarriages, one scheduled surgery on my left ovary and one emergency surgery to remove my left tube, and I have had two near-death experiences. There's a lot to discuss, but before we get to all that, let me provide a brief history on how Joe and I came to be married and how we ended up where we are today.

We met in November 1999, the week after Thanksgiving, right before the whole Y2K drama. That was a fun time. People were stocking up on everything from portable grills to camping gear to water; it still makes me chuckle when I think back on it. Anyway, Joe and I knew the same people and had even attended the same parties, but we had actually never met. Then, one night in November, one of our mutual friends had a big birthday party, and we were both at that party. We ended up meeting somehow and spent the rest of the evening talking with each other. As my girlfriends and I were leaving, Joe walked us to my car and asked for my phone number. Before I knew it, one of my friends had already written it down on a piece of paper and was waving it in her hand out the passenger side window.

After dating for a couple of years, we tied the knot in May 2003. We closed the chapter in our lives of being separate individuals and started a new chapter of living life together. We both had big dreams for our future, and, naturally, we wanted to get our ducks in a row and plan for what we thought would be our perfect life—boy, were we in for a shock! You see, before Joe and I met, we were not interested in pursuing our education. We both had taken a few classes at the local community college here and there out of high school. We did not take education seriously, nor the discipline it brings. Joe was twenty-seven years old, I was twenty-six, and we were young, careless, and stupid. Like I said, I could write a whole book on our lives before we met, but let me stay on track.

By the time we married, we had earned our associates degrees, Joe in information services, me in general studies. We were both working full-time, and we quickly realized we would need a formal education if we were going to move up in the world. We decided to pursue our bachelor's degrees, and, with the Lord's guidance, Joe obtained his Bachelor of Science in information technology, and I received mine in finance (I graduated Cum Laude). While it took us both a very long time, we continued our education and completed graduate studies as well. Joe earned his Master of Science (MS) in the same field, while I obtained my MS in business, with a concentration in finance. We both attended University of Maryland school systems, and talk about completely turning our lives around! We are living, breathing testaments of how God can change you utterly around, in every aspect.

We were well on our way and on the right track at last. We had both partied and lived careless lives, and we paid for it by being broke and by spending all our time either working, attending classes, or studying. For nearly eight years we did not have time to go out or hang out with old friends, let alone go on vacation. It takes longer to obtain degrees when you work full time and can only attend classes on a part-time basis. We both used our vacation days from work to study for finals, writing papers or finalizing projects. While we were busting our rumps to "get ahead" in life, it was a memorable, even enjoyable, time. I thank the Lord He gave us the perseverance and motivation to complete our graduate studies. What I enjoyed most was attending class; I really liked learning, and I was happy.

By May of 2008, I was finished with school. We both had good paying jobs, and we had joined a Presbyterian church. We decided we were ready to start a family. We had no idea of the complications, hurt, pain, and confusion that would await us

Chapter 1

year after year, for the next five years. At the time, we were bright eyed and ready, and we embarked on this journey full of hope and expectation. I was taught, and thought I wanted, to climb the corporate ladder. I was a debutante ready to enter corporate America and was hungry to achieve and to earn a big salary, and this is where the real story begins.

Chapter 2

Our plan was to graduate, get good jobs, buy a house, and then start a family. Sounds simple and innocent enough, so I stopped taking my birth control pills in June 2008, and wouldn't you know it, I got pregnant in January 2009—YAY! Whew, talk about waiting to get pregnant. I was ready to start a family right away, and I had to wait an agonizing seven months before getting pregnant. Honestly, I don't remember how I found out I was pregnant, as in if I took a pregnancy test at home or if I had missed my cycle and gone to the doctor for confirmation, but we were happy, and I was pregnant. Oh, the Lord is so good when things go according to our plans, especially on our timelines. Not only was I pregnant, I was able to land a new job, an even higher paying job, at a big name corporation.

After some time getting a bit of experience at a bank, I was able to land a great job at a well-known hospital in Baltimore, Maryland. I learned a lot there, but I was ready to move on after a year and a half. I couldn't put my finger on it back then, but the Lord was teaching me that my dependence on myself was distancing me from Him. This job at the hospital was a highly sought after position, and people all over the world wanted to work there. By God's grace, I was selected. I should have been happy—this is why I decided to get an education—but I wasn't. You see, this medical facility is world renowned, and during the very first hour of orientation, we were pumped full of messages about how "great" we all were and that we were the "best of the best," and I started to believe it. Naturally, I started developing a big head and giving myself credit for how awesome I was. I decided I needed to think even higher of myself, so I began applying to various firms, and wouldn't you know it, a government defense contractor offered me a job.

At first I was ecstatic. Not only would I be getting an even higher salary, this corporation was closer to home, which meant a shorter commute, and I would no longer need to pay monthly parking fees as I had working in Baltimore. This company was huge, I was moving up in the world, and my life was going just where I thought it was supposed to go. Like I said, at first I was ecstatic, but then I rapidly lost that sense of delight. In retrospect, the challenge and excitement for me was obtaining the next position, the next level up, the acceptance and affirmation that I was good enough for that company and to fulfill that role. I thought if I could just land that job, I would be sure I was good enough, and after that, I could be happy. Of course, it did not work out that way because once I was offered the position and was earning more money, all of a sudden, I felt I wasn't making enough, and I had to work at getting more.

I was a few months into working with the defense contractor when the Department of Defense came knocking. In my mad search to leave the hospital, the government was one of places I had applied to. I thought if I could land a job in this federal government agency, I would have finally arrived and would need to search no more. Once I got in, I would stay put for good and finally be happy. This was the opportunity of a lifetime, and I took it. It took quite a while for me to actually start with the government, but in the meantime, things were looking up in my life. I was employed with the defense contractor, making more money, working on a few interesting projects, and above all, I was pregnant. I thanked God and thought, *You are so good to me, You must really love me.*

Joe was still a new Christian when we married in May 2003. He had repented and accepted Jesus as his Lord and Savior a couple of years before and was baptized soon after. I had accepted Christ as my Savior in the second grade but was not baptized until I was twenty-nine years old. I'll never forget that moment, that lesson in elementary school, when I became saved. I was attending Arlington Baptist Church and School in Baltimore. It was a small private Christian school, and when I look back on it now, I realize it was a great school.

One of the subjects was Bible Study, and chorus was mandatory. We were required to memorize Bible verses, and we sang beautiful songs. Our choir competed against other schools and often did very well. We all wore uniforms: girls wore dresses or skirts and boys wore slacks. Our colors were white and green. My second grade teacher was Mrs. Redmiles, and she is the one who led me to Christ. She gave a lesson during Bible Study one random day, and she said that if we wanted to go to heaven, we had to repent and ask Jesus to come into our hearts.

For some reason, I was hypnotized. Mind you, I was in the second grade, and I still remember this vividly. This had been my second year at the school, and I had heard about Jesus before, but I did not really understand—or care, for that matter. During that particular Bible Study class, Mrs. Redmiles said that if we wanted to stay after class a few minutes to give our lives to Jesus, she would help us pray. I was a little hesitant. What would my parents think? They were Buddhists. What would my brothers and sister think? They attended the same school, but we were all just attending this school because our parents had placed us there. My parents wanted for us to be Buddhists; we were only attending a private school because they heard it was a good school. Little did they know I would become the first Christian in the family.

My one brother, Brian, is five years older than me so he was in the seventh grade. My other brother, Kenny, is seven years older, and he was in the ninth grade at the time with my sister, Kay, being in the eleventh grade. The elementary section of the school was in a separate building, on the other side of the campus, so I never saw them in school. As a matter of fact, we all rode the same bus, but I never recall them being on the bus either. It's probably because the younger kids sat in the front, while the cool older students sat in the back.

So after the Bible Study class, we were whisked away to our next class. There were several subjects afterward, but I could not get the feeling of wanting to go to heaven out of my head. Even as a second grader, it kept nagging me. After the last class of the day, we had approximately ten minutes to get to our bus. After the last class, instead of walking my normal route to my bus, I ran back to Mrs. Redmiles's class. She asked me why I wasn't on my bus, and I asked her if she could help me go to heaven. Again, I was seven years old at the time; this is more than thirty years ago, and I still remember this day. A big, loving smile came across Mrs. Redmiles's face, and she asked me to repeat after her. She said that if I meant what I would say with my whole heart, Jesus would come into my heart.

The prayer went something like, "Dear Jesus, I am a sinner. Please forgive me my sins. Please wash me white as snow. Please come and live in my heart as I want to live in heaven with You forever." I repeated after Mrs. Redmiles, and I truly did mean it with my whole heart. We ended with, "In Jesus' name, amen."

When I opened my eyes, Mrs. Redmiles gave me a big hug and said, "Now you get to go to heaven!" I was so happy, I remember feeling better than on Christmas morning. Then she said, "Now run to your bus!" When I walked out of her classroom, I thought all the kids would be on their buses by now and that perhaps I even missed my bus, but in fact, I walked outside, and it was the normal scurrying and scampering as all the kids were running to their buses, as if time had stood still.

I ran to my bus, found a seat next to my friend, and told her what had happened. I don't remember her name, but she said, "Oh, yay!"

Mrs. Redmiles, I never did thank you for leading me to Christ. Thank you for your teaching that day. Thank you for loving me enough to pray with me. I pray I can thank you in person; if not in this life, be on the lookout for me in heaven. Because I became saved that day, I was able to pray for my parents to become Christians. I prayed for over fifteen years, and praise God, they are saved today!

My family did give me hard time when I came home that day and confessed I had become a Christian and would be going to heaven. My siblings made fun of me while my parents began plotting ways to undo all this Jesus stuff. I still have my Bible from elementary school, and my sister recorded the day I got saved in my Bible. I did love the Lord when I first became saved. At age seven I would ask strangers if they knew Jesus. On the playground I would ask the children and their parents if they were Christians and would explain how Jesus died for our sins and that all we needed to do was pray with our whole hearts, confess our sins, and ask Jesus to come into our hearts, then we could live in heaven forever.

I had very vivid dreams of Jesus as a child. For instance, on my eighth birthday, I dreamed that Jesus came to my birthday party. He descended from the ceiling, and I ran up and gave Him a hug and thanked Him profusely for attending my birthday party. Jesus gave me a present, and when I opened the box, it was a pair of bright white gloves. I didn't even know I liked gloves, but I was so happy to receive them that I put them on right away. Jesus said, "Promise me you will not take off these gloves," and I promised that I would never, ever take them off. Of course, I completely lied, and those white gloves came flying off a long time ago. However, thanks be to God, even though I have lived for myself and completely defied my King, He forgave me, will continue to forgive me, and promises to forgive me in the future—thank You, Jesus.

So while I had accepted Christ as my Savior at the age of seven, I had lived a completely non-Christian life until I got married. First of all, my parents were Buddhists, so Monday through Friday I had a Christian influence in school, which I really liked. Then on Saturdays, my parents would take me to the Buddhist monk to undo all that Christian stuff. I had no idea what my parents and the monk were saying; it was all in Korean, and by that time, I couldn't understand half of their conversations. Needless to say, I'm really good at tuning things out as a result of my childhood. My parents would take them an envelope full of cash. They would bow down in front of the Buddhist statues, and they even brought food to the temple.

On those Saturday voyages, the Buddhist monk would sit me on his lap and tell me to call him "Father." He would say to me, "Su, tell me that I'm your father." I felt very uncomfortable with that, but I did it anyway since my parents were there giving me threatening looks. Thankfully, after some time, my parents stopped taking me, and my aunt started taking me to church with her on Sundays. I had grown up in some type of church environment after my Saturday stints with the monks, but I never really understood what God was about or what it meant to have a relationship with Him. My understanding of God was that He was mad at me when I lied, misbehaved or was anything but a good girl.

As a young child and growing up in my teens and onward, I was living my life how I wanted, going through the motions, and especially in my late teen years, early twenties, living a reckless, dangerous, and wasteful life. The bold defiance and utter recklessness of the lifestyle I lived is shameful, and yet God still loved me and never gave up on me. When I met Joe, we started attending a Presbyterian church in Baltimore. It was a good start for our Christian walk together. We were both baptized there, but we still had a long way to go. After a couple of years, we decided to find a new church closer to home. The Lord brought us to Columbia Presbyterian Church (CPC) in Columbia, Maryland, which is where our walk with Christ really took off.

We attended CPC for about eight years, living, growing, and

maturing in Christ. This time is also when the toughest five years of our lives happened. As I said, I got pregnant in January 2009. This is what we had planned, and things were going according to our schedule. I was working for a government defense contractor at the time and was waiting to start my new job with the federal government. I was thirty-three years old, had turned my life around, was getting closer to Christ, and Joe and I were on our way to becoming parents. We were living the good life, with baby in tow soon enough. Next item on the list of things to accomplish was checked off. All was well.

Chapter 3

Things were going swimmingly; God was blessing us so! I would be starting my new job with the federal government in one month, making even more money, and I had passed all the stringent background scrutiny. I felt reaffirmed of my worth for being accepted to the agency, and Joe was moving up the corporate ladder as well. Little did I know my world was about to crumble, and not only that, but stay there for the next five years. I was approximately nine and half weeks pregnant, when one morning, I was at work, as usual. It was March 16, 2009, and nothing too out of the ordinary was occurring. Joe was at work as well, and we had our regularly scheduled check-up later that afternoon. While I was at work, I went to the bathroom. I had started spotting. It was light pink, and it had just started. I did not think anything was wrong, but since my OB wanted me to call if anything out of the ordinary occurred, I decided to call my doctor rather than waiting to see her later that day.

    The doctor's office asked me to come in sooner than our scheduled appointment so I asked my manager if I could leave sooner than my requested departure time, and he, of course, agreed. I called Joe at work to explain what was going on, and he was leaving work as well to meet me at the doctor's office. We were both there within the hour. By this time, the spotting had gotten darker red and was more than a spot. They had me undress, put on the standard hospital gown, and lay down on the examining table. I was little worried, but I thought it was something they would dismiss and that I was worrying for nothing. Joe said I looked really cute laying there, and I just chuckled as we waited for someone to come back in the room.

The first technician came in and conducted a sonogram. She was looking and poking around and not saying anything. She then called in a second technician; they were pointing to the screen, giving each other nods, then they both left without saying a word other than that the doctor would be in shortly. The doctor came in, and I was thinking how both technicians were pretty rude and did not even try to offer an explanation as to what was going on. The doctor conducted her own sonogram when she entered the room and then finally said, "We can't find it."

Joe said, "You can't find what?"

The doctor went on to explain that at this point in the pregnancy, the embryo should be this big and right here, pointing to the place on the monitor where the baby should be.

She kept poking around, and again she said, "It's not here." I did not fully understand what this meant. I was lying on the examining bed, and she started explaining how I would need to be scheduled for a D&C. I did not know what this was, but I knew I did not want it. I tuned out what she said next. She and Joe started having a conversation. I was thinking to myself that they were mistaken, my baby was there. I thought I needed to find another doctor to get a second opinion.

They asked Joe and me to think about it at home, and I can remember saying to Joe, "Maybe it'll come back and show up." My doctor said that if I did not lose it naturally, they would schedule the D&C to ensure it was completely removed. We went home, and I was worried, to say the least. I was confused, unsure, and I kept thinking the little guy/gal was there and would show up tomorrow. Joe said he would stay at home with me the rest of the afternoon, but I convinced him to go back to work since I didn't know what was happening. Plus, I needed time alone to think and process what this all meant. I did not realize I was going through a miscarriage.

If you have never experienced a miscarriage, the physical pain

Chapter 3

of losing the baby is horrible and excruciating. I have always had really bad menstrual cramps, and I thought those were bad! No, having a miscarriage is unlike any other. Not only do you know the baby is physically detaching itself, which again is very painful, it takes an emotional toll as well, knowing that the little baby is dead and leaving you. I was saying to the baby, "I'm sorry, little one, that I didn't take better care of you or myself. Please don't leave." I don't want to get too graphic, but there was a lot of pain and a lot of blood. I was in too much pain during the actual miscarriage to call Joe. Afterward, I called Joe to tell him I had lost the baby. He came home right away and lay next to me in bed while I fell asleep.

We had a dog, Rusty, my sweet boy, Rusty. He knew something was wrong with me the moment we walked in the house from the doctor's office. Normally, he wags his tail and wants us to pet him and tell him he's a good boy, which he certainly was; he was the best. Typically, he would go back to his bed or play with his ball after a couple of minutes of getting attention. But that afternoon when we walked in, he started wagging his tail as usual, but it slowed, and he came and sat right next to me. Usually, after I pet Rusty, I'll go fumble around with something in the kitchen, or go upstairs to change my clothes, but this day, I walked in, went straight to the couch, and sat down. While I sat on the couch thinking about what was happening, Rusty came and put his face in my lap. He put his adorable chin on my knee; he was looking up at me with his sweet brown eyes, and that's when I started crying.

I hugged Rusty and thanked him for trying to make me feel better. I sat there just crying and asking God, "WHY?!" Rusty lay by my feet, and I felt as if God had Rusty lay there, just letting me know that He was with me, comforting me. Jesus said, "I have told you these things, so that in me you may have peace. In this world you will have trouble. But take heart! I have overcome the world." (John 16:33) In the back of my mind, I knew this and remembered this verse; however, like Peter, rather than keeping my gaze on Jesus, I was easily distracted by my present troubles, and I sank deep into them.

It is safe to say I was not feeling at peace during that time. I was in physical pain, emotional turmoil, and in a general state of uncertainty about everything. Our plans were not being fulfilled; we were going to get married, finish school, find good jobs, and then start a family. Miscarriage was nowhere in our plans; actually, that notion never even crossed my mind. Who in the world has a miscarriage? That is something that happens to someone else, it happens to your neighbor's daughter's best friend, or you read about it in a magazine as something that happens to someone else, but not to you.

Up until that point, I had never directly known anyone who had gone through a miscarriage. Again, I had heard about others going through it, but honestly, I had never really thought about what actually happens when a woman miscarries. Even after all of my losses and speaking to other women, this is not a topic that is discussed. A couple of women whom I did speak with that had experienced losses were very quick to change the topic. It is almost shunned and taboo to speak of. It's such a private matter and an embarrassing one. Who in the world can't keep a baby to full term? Me, apparently, and I felt very alone. I've always had a difficult time expressing my feelings, especially when I am sad or mad. I just can't think straight when I am disheveled.

In order for me to process how I feel, I need to be able to label it, put a word on it, and I can't do that until after the event. I realize now that it takes me time to process my sadness, and I am unable to communicate my feelings until I do. Because I did not know how to describe what was going on as well as unsure of how I was supposed to feel, I felt extremely isolated. Joe was the closest person I had in my life, and I was unable to talk to him about it. I did not have the words to appropriately capture what I was going through. It's as if trying to describe a color to a blind person, and the color I could not describe was gray. Where do I start? How do I describe feeling nothing? My words seemed to diminish what I was feeling, and no word was good enough, so I said nothing.

Chapter 3

From March 16 to April 10, 2009, I was a zombie, the dead among the living. I did not know how to feel, what to think, what to do or how to begin the process of healing. March 16 was a Monday, the day I miscarried. I took off Tuesday, of course, but I went right back to work on Wednesday, March 18. At work, I was fine on the outside; no one knew I had been pregnant or had just lost my baby. Only my manager knew, and he kept saying to me, "Take all the time you need." I thought if I didn't think about it and just buried myself in work, my feelings would work themselves out and everything would go back to normal. I had no idea on what to do for myself. I still did not understand why I lost our baby, and I didn't have any answers.

I was about to start my new job with the Department of Defense. All my background and clearance information checked out, and I was scheduled to start my new job on Monday, April 13, 2009. I felt as if I needed to get myself together and appear normal at work, especially since I would be starting a new job in less than one month. Over the course of the next year, I became depressed and physically unable to enjoy life. I went to work, came home, sat or lay on my couch, ate, and watched television. That was my life for a year. I didn't cook, clean, go out, or do much of anything. I still attended church, family gatherings, and holiday events, and on the surface I was fine, but on the inside, I was empty.

One thing that kept me going was that God never let me go. I was not holding onto Him—or anything for that matter—He was holding me. It helps to have distractions, such as starting a new job. That in itself is stressful, and where I worked, my full attention was needed while at work. But at home, I had a very inner sadness that I didn't think much about. It robbed me of all enthusiasm, excitement, and fun. Having a good time just did not matter to me. I was content on the couch, eating, and watching TV. When I think back on it now, I never knew I was depressed until I got better. People tend to think that just because something is not working out, they need to accept it and think, "Oh well, that's my life." But no, it does not need to be. God wants us to be at peace, content, and living joyfully.

He wants that so much for us that He sent His one and only son, whom He loves, to earth in order to provide all the peace, comfort, and joy every single one of us will ever need. It never runs out; as a matter of fact, His grace is new and renews each morning. The first step in accepting this type of life is to acknowledge we want that. We have free will to make our own decisions, and we need to decide that we want a better life. God wants us to have a great life, and in fact, He made it possible for us. However, we need to take that first step and admit we want that life for ourselves.

During that year on the couch, I was not living, nor admitting that I wanted a better life. I gained twenty pounds and hated myself more than ever. I've always struggled with weight, and it's been in constant flux since I was a little girl. The more I ate, the more weight I gained, and the more I disliked myself and my life. But God is so good, He allowed my husband, Joe, to sit, eat, and watch television with me every step of the way. Never once did Joe make me feel bad about myself. He was positive, loving, and so patient with me. Joe hung out with me, made me laugh, and even got me walking with him and Rusty. I thank God that He gave me Joe and Rusty to show His love for me through them.

For me personally, I learned that watching television is not healthy. It often left me feeling inadequate and uneasy. There is a lot of drama and distractions, and television has a cunning way of telling you that what you have is not enough. I started out watching dramas and reality shows, but I realized what I saw and heard made a lasting impression on me and my outlook on life and people. The Holy Spirit guided me to start watching less of the drama and more on history, arts, nature, wildlife, and Christian programs. I started to feel less disheveled as I tuned into more educational programs. Today, I hardly watch anything on television, other than *Duck Dynasty*, and most of what we watch is about nature, animals, religion, or some other topics of interest. We do like watching movies, but we have even started limiting our movie watching to those that are less disturbing.

Chapter 3

Joe bought me a guitar, keyboard, writing desk, notebooks, and pens. He didn't know what would help me, but he kept trying. Through it all, I cried and prayed, a lot, and so did Joe. Eventually, I started writing and putting all my thoughts on paper. Actually, a couple of days after I miscarried, I was led to write this poem. After I wrote this, I fell off the earth spiritually and emotionally for one month:

My God is Sovereign

In every single step, my God is there
God's hand is in everywhere

No matter what my plans or dreams I behold,
My Father in heaven dictates His will to unfold

Although I don't know why it seems this way,
All I can do is still praise Him, the rest of my days

So I look to the cross,
Where my Lord and Savior died,
And thank Him for my punishment He bore,
That one day I'll be with Him,
In heaven, right before my very eyes

Thank You, Father, that one day you'll call us home,
To sing, to laugh, to dance and celebrate,
Oh, that day, what a perfect one it will be,
To be with You eternally,
And no more yearning there shall be.

My God, I know You are sovereign,
That is all, that is the end, there is no other way,
My Father in heaven, my Lord and my King.

Chapter 4

For some reason, I e-mailed that poem to our church prayer chain, and anyone who knows me knows I do not express my feelings very well, especially sadness. I believe the Holy Spirit was working through me to share my poem, and after I hit the send button, love poured in from church. I received phone calls, cards, food left at my doorstep, and spontaneous hugs of support at church. While this helped in my healing process, I was a long way from Wellville.

    I heard so many comments, from, "You'll be fine next time" to "I lost my first one too" to "I can't believe you told everybody about it" to "Have you tried ____." Fill in the blank, and I have heard it all. The comments came from both church-going women and secular women. I started to resent anyone sharing their comments with me; I just wanted everyone to shut up. What do they know? They appeared to be living happy lives, with kids, and no one understood what I was going through. I'll never forget one lady told me not to speak of it; this was something that I buried deep, deep down inside and never let out. I was angry, sad, frustrated, bitter, embarrassed, overweight, and the only pinprick of light in that darkness that held me was my writing to God about it.

    After my miscarriage, I had stomach cramps for a couple of weeks following the loss. I prayed for God to heal me completely, and even more, that He would change my heart. I was starting

Chapter 4

my new job, and I was worried I would not be able to wholly engage myself due to being distracted by the lingering cramps.

As I said, a few days after I miscarried, I wrote "My God is Sovereign," then I went completely blank for a month. With Joe loving and praying for me, I decided to start writing again. I started on April 10, 2009, which happened to be Good Friday that year. It's strange that I can feel so low, sad, and unmotivated, yet I loved God and knew He loved me. It was such an oxymoron; I knew I would go to heaven if Jesus came back, yet I was unhappy. I realize now that I did not allow myself time to heal, to understand what going through a miscarriage meant, and that it was okay for me to feel sad.

That Sunday, April 12, was Easter Sunday (He is risen, He is risen, indeed!). I was starting my new job with the Department of Defense the next day. Thank the good Lord, I was all healed physically, and I would be able to start my new job without the baggage of being distracted. But I did carry the emotional baggage with me, which can be just as bad, maybe even worse.

It is safe to say that the Lord led us to CPC to help us grow spiritually and be mature enough to go through what we went through. If I had gone through these losses at any time before, I would have ended up drinking and doing drugs again to help me forget. Instead, I experienced each loss, looked at it straight on with tearful eyes and clutched hands, but with my Christ in view. There's no doubt about it, I was sad and hurting deeply within; however, heavenly hands gently carried me through. I wrote this that Easter, the day before I started my new job with the government:

Oh, Father, how I love You, and how I pray to be stronger in You.
To love no matter what comes my way
To love no matter what others might say
To love no matter the temptation to stray
To love You, Father,
More, in You.

Our Father in heaven is glorious! How can anyone resist His love? It is because they do not know Him. I pray this one story of a Christian couple, from a small town, will bring just one more to your banquet table, Lord.

It was quite a while before I wrote again. In fact, it was the next year, May 4, 2010. While I wanted nothing more than to forget my losses, I was compelled to keep track of them for some reason. I don't have a written account of this loss as to the exact date, but around September or October 2009, I was pregnant for a few weeks and then lost another baby. I had taken a home pregnancy test, and it was positive. I wanted to wait a few more weeks before calling my doctor, as it was very early in the pregnancy. Only, after three weeks, I miscarried this one too while I was at home. No one knew but me and Joe.

This loss compounded my insecurities, as I was still holding on to the first loss. I was beginning to think that my body was cursed. I was being punished for the drinking and drugs I had done in my party years. Mind you, while I knew for a fact that Jesus came to earth and died for all my sins on the cross, I still thought I was being punished. Talk about being misguided! I was in such an internal battle for my happiness, and sadness had been winning for over a year.

The second loss reaffirmed my depression. There would be times when I would be freed from thinking about having a baby, or the loss of one, and I would experience pockets of freedom as I tried to forget my first miscarriage, my hurt, and struggles with life in general. Usually, those times were when we would go on a trip, but even then, there was a thin film that filtered those good times through my "woe is me" goggles. But this second loss confirmed that I was being held captive by gloom, and there was no use in trying to escape anymore. I was in prison and even tried to convince myself I belonged in the shadows, but God was there and kept sparking life in me.

For the past five years, I have had miscarriages or surgeries around March or April and also had two losses in September or

Chapter 4

October each year. I was afraid that my body was remembering it expelling something around those times each year and would continue to do so. It's crazy and maddening to think of all the "what ifs" that can happen to you or a loved one. The enemy is the chief distracter, accuser, and destroyer. If I am not careful, I can easily slip into my tendencies of hopelessness. I need to catch myself and pray immediately to refocus my purpose and thoughts on the completed work of Jesus Christ on the cross.

While I am better today, there are still thoughts, actions, and interactions that try my contentment in Jesus. To get me back on the narrow road to life (Matthew 7:13), I literally start reading scripture and praying afterward. I pray for those around me and for myself, and if someone wronged me in some way, I ask the Lord to bless them. For me, no amount of medication, exercise, self-talk, or any other self-prescribed actions makes me feel instantly at peace and keeping on with what I need to do than reading the Bible and praying to God, and trust me, I've tried it all.

In the past, if someone did or said something to me that I thought was wrong, that interaction would keep replaying in my mind. I would think that I should've said something back or behaved differently. It was especially hard to be in the present when I kept thinking about the babies I had lost. It would take me out of the present and back into an event that occurred in the past, and that is no way to live. Because I lived that way for so long, I can easily detect when I start slipping away from the present, and I immediately take it to God in prayer. And wouldn't you know it, today I am able to be more satisfied living in the present. I am able to have more fun and laugh more being in the present. Thank You, Jesus.

For those who may be thinking, "Yeah, that's fine and all, but I need something real and tangible to help me," let me tell you, there is nothing more real and tangible than reading the Bible and visualizing what Jesus had to go through. Once you train your mind to keep your thoughts on "whatever is true, whatever is noble, whatever is right, whatever is pure, whatever is lovely, whatever is admirable, if anything is excellent or praiseworthy—think about such things" (Philippians 4:8), the painful memories and vicious thoughts do leave. If you have never tried it or things keep haunting you—angry feelings, frustrated plans—try visualizing what God did for us. It will take a real, concerted effort the first few times, but afterward, it does become easier, like any new goal.

Think about it—God and Jesus existed before time began, before the earth was formed. They were in perfect peace and love. Once man and woman were created, sinned, and creation fell; mankind continued to spiral down to despair. But God loved us so much, He sent his son to earth. Jesus left heaven, His glorious throne, to come down to earth to be with us. He came to earth knowing He would die the most painful death, even though He was completely innocent. Jesus came to show us that He is the way and the life. He conquered death and hell so we can live eternally with Him. What else does He need to do in order for us to believe Him? What has He not done? I wrote this in December 2008 as I pondered what Christmas meant:

What is Christmas?

What is Christmas, but just another day,
When subtle nuisances are temporarily put away?

But why? So joyful on the surface due to spirits and gifts,
That afterward, we realize how desperately hopeless we are,
Fooled yet again by the holiday myths.

It's not our fault, everyone else is so wrapped in up the season.
We too are often swept up and forget the true reason.

Thankfully, not every speck of dust is brushed away.
Some remain, refrain, and do not stray.
Not by our willingness or might,
But by the grace of God who provided the cover,
That we may proclaim, **Not without a fight!**

Chapter 4

What is a speck to do, so unreliable, so untrue,
That oftentimes the pressure to be wiped away does prevail.
So Jesus came to be a speck among us and to save,
All while listening to the other specks grumble and wail.

God said, I love you too much, so I shall have my son pave the way.

How in the world can this be? My Lord and Savior was a speck, just like me!
By His loving light it is made known it wasn't of this world, but from heaven this is,
And this gift is free.

My Father's irresistible love, the celebration of my living Savior's birth,
And the Holy Spirit left as a deposit for me...

This is what Christmas is.

The precious gift, courtesy of Jesus,
That is for everyone, not just us.

Until the time I am allowed to be lifted from this earthly dust cloud,
May I continually offer up my heart, my soul, my love,
Not only for You to see,

But that the rest of the world may know, Jesus is why we say Merry Christmas,
'til the end of time as You intend it to be.

Love, this is what Christmas is.

Chapter 5

By May 2010, I had been with the government for over a year and had had two miscarriages since March 2009. I had started writing again, and I forged friendships with a few women from church and work. Every single month since I first became pregnant in January 2009, I was hoping I would be pregnant the next month. It is agonizing waiting each month. Month after month I would stay away from caffeine, sushi, alcohol or anything I thought might jeopardize a potential pregnancy. Then, when I would realize I was not pregnant, I would have coffee, sushi, alcohol, and anything else I wanted. It was no way to live. I read and read to try to understand what the culprit might be. Ideas and thoughts turned into pondering and daydreaming until I became obsessed with having a baby.

I experienced firsthand how sin slowly takes over your entire life and body. It seems so innocent at first, and initially, whatever you're doing probably is. The enemy roams around looking to devour someone, to have sin take over, as that is what his mission is, to keep us distracted. At this time in my life, there were about seven other women I knew of trying to get pregnant as well. While I appreciated knowing I was not the only one who couldn't get pregnant, I was the only one in the group who had experienced miscarriages. Eventually, it got to the point where I did not want to hear the other women discussing their infertility issues. Also, by the same time the following year, most of them had delivered babies.

A few conceived naturally, others through IVF or some other form of professional assistance. They would say to me, "Just stop thinking about it and it'll happen." It made me sigh, as they would not have wanted to hear that a year earlier, and here they had already forgotten what it felt like. I guess that is true with most any experience you pull through. As I look back now and think about all my losses, it was very sad, embarrassing and painful, yet I find that opening up about how sad I felt overall is the most challenging part for me to write about.

However, God is so good that His healing trumps my doubts, His love overcomes my sadness, His strength towers over my weaknesses, and I cannot help but acclaim His powerful work, regardless of how self-conscious I feel. That is how I know the Holy Spirit is working in me, because if it were up to me, I'd be self-healing through some twelve-step process, drinking, or through some other worldly way. While that may help me temporarily, and it has, nothing has genuinely healed me, or as thoroughly, from deep within my heart and exuding out to my fingertips and toes. But before I was able to let go and let God work, I struggled with all kinds of sin. Like I said, I even turned something as harmless as wanting to start a family into an ugly, all out, completely engrossing sin.

Sin's Tale

Shh! Wait, do you hear that? Quiet, be still and listen. There's something there…

There it is. It sounds like the branches on a tree, stretching its long, scraggly fingers, its jagged fingernails subtly scratching against the glass window.

The faint tapping and scratches have stopped. Whew, now I can relax and get on with what I was doing. Huh? Am I hearing something again? Knock, knock. "Who's there?"

BANG! BANG! BANG! "Who is pounding on my door?" I walk outside and have blended in with the crowd.

A needle has pricked my heart. Since it only hurt for a second, I'll ignore it.

The pricking of a needle point has transformed itself from the slightest of pressures into this mangled metal claw, gripping and piercing into my fleshy heart. The sharp metal claws have attached itself onto my heart, like my heart grew a fifth chamber. Only, rather than giving me additional life, this is draining my life away.

I acted to feed that sin, and now it has a grip on my heart, and it won't let go.

Father, I beg you, remove this sin from me. Cut it out of my heart so that it may be mended with your healing love.

Lord, it was my sin that you were freeing my heart and soul from. The cold metal sharp claws that you bore, that was clamped onto your entire body, my sin that was slashed across your back, my flagrant disregard that pounded the nails into your hands and feet. Your broken body poured out the blood that conquered sin and defeated death once and for all.

Thank You, Lord, for allowing me to be in your presence one day, I pray I will keep my sights on you. In Jesus' name is all things said, healed, forgiven, and done, amen.

I started seeing an acupuncturist to help me. He was a retired pastor who lost his first wife to cancer. He started studying acupuncture when his first wife became ill in hopes of healing her through prayer and needles. Somehow, my parents found out about him and so Joe and I started seeing him. At first we went to see him for seasonal allergies. I had terrible seasonal allergies, so much so I was on two prescription-strength allergy medicines every single day, and on days it was really bad, took over-the-counter head cold medicine as well.

My body was getting used to the two prescription-strength medicines, so I was being rotated onto new medicine every couple of years. Thank the good Lord, the pastor was able to help me with my seasonal allergies and the acupuncture and herbal teas helped get me off my prescription meds. I haven't been on regular prescription-strength allergy medication for several years now. I still take prescription nasal spray every now and then, maybe a couple of times per month, but certainly not every day. Since he helped with my allergies, I confided in him about my miscarriages. He started "treating" me for infertility and miscarriages as well.

During this time, I clung on to the following verse: "Trust in the Lord with all your heart, lean not on your own understanding; in all your ways submit to Him, and He will make your paths straight." (Proverbs 3: 5–6) Even though I was still stressing out about becoming pregnant, still hurt and mad, I earnestly wanted to have inner peace and for love to fill my heart, I just didn't know how to go about getting that. I was torn and having such a hard time healing emotionally. Turbulent childhood memories haunted me, the anger and fear I felt growing up, the uncertainty of knowing how to feel during stressful times, and yet, I so wanted to have the true contentment that comes with knowing Christ.

I needed to resolve all my issues of feeling hurt, afraid, confused, and overall not knowing how to feel. It made me wonder how some women knew exactly what to say, how to feel, and what to do. I was so far from that. Here I was, about to turn thirty-five in a few months, and I didn't even know if my feelings were right. Every time I was angry, sad or frustrated, I would doubt myself and wonder, *Do I have a right to feel this way?* Needless to say, I was in inner turmoil and having miscarriages didn't help. The common thread throughout these difficult years, and the losses, was that Jesus was right next to me.

In Jesus' Name

In Jesus' name we come
It's only in His name we may live

Thank You, Father, for the Spirit
By Your grace it is how we accept what You freely give

You say you will make our paths straight,
How many will come, how many will doubt?
Even I, a supposed believer, need reminding that indeed You
And You alone are great

Father, help me to trust You in every single one of my ways
To not trust my own understanding, but to my Savior I turn,
That You alone would hold my gaze

I give You all my heart and pray Your will be done
Spirit, guide me on the righteous journey
Until the day Your victory is eternally won.

While I am healing, growing, and maturing, I realize at this stage in my life I am in perpetual spiritual puberty. I am struggling to show the fruits of the Spirit, even though that is what I truly wanted. I am so angry with everyone. I am angry and impatient with Joe, my family members, coworkers, and strangers. I can barely stand myself. I start pondering Proverbs 1:7, "The fear of the Lord is the beginning of knowledge, but fools despise wisdom and discipline."

Chapter 5

Because of You

I am here, at this moment, solely because of You
Not by my hand or by some coincidental circumstance

It is Your plan and will that has brought me here
I pray I will learn, listen, and follow
And not live life as if by some happen chance

Father, I am here and I will go where You send me
If You say we are not to be fruitful,
Then, Lord, I will still love You and bend my knee

Help me to want You alone; my whole heart is Yours
No matter what may come, I can say it is well

I will search for You behind every door
And say boldly, **Father, is this your will?**

And patiently wait while loving You more,
Secure in knowing eventually with You eternally I will dwell.

Chapter 6

It is June 2010, I'll be thirty-five in July, and I still want to have children. I must be crazy; that's the only explanation. I have simply lost it and am out of my mind. It's been a little over a year since I started my job with the Department of Defense and again, I feel as if I need to move on and move up. I dislike the environment I'm in, and I don't know why I am not content. I am supposed to be happy, I have a good and expensive education, have worked my way up to this government agency, and yet, with every new and "better" job, I feel something is really lacking. I feel like I don't belong here. I've worked at great companies so far, with each job and new company; it certainly is viewed as a step up in the world's view. I was doing what people are supposed to do, get a job with a good company and make a lot of money. Why do I have such a dismal outlook?

What was strange was that when I was having lunch with girlfriends, attending family gatherings or church events, I seemed fine enough on the outside. People probably thought I was a bit strange, as no matter how I wanted to conceal my unhappiness, one's true sentiment pours out in other ways. Joe did not know how unhappy I truly was. He knew I was still sad from the losses, and he thought I was going through the healing process, which I was, but I was healing from more than my losses. Joe was busy with work, working on his cars, and taking care of

Chapter 6

Rusty. After the interactions and gatherings I had with family and friends, I would go back home and pick up where I left off, sitting on my couch and just feeling blah.

I continued on year after year as that is what I thought I was supposed to do. The standard of living had been ingrained, and I was living it, only I did not realize it was not the life for me. I kept ignoring my inner voice, suppressing and repressing what I really wanted. I was still unsure as to what I wanted, but I knew I did not feel comfortable with myself. We lived in one of the most exclusive counties in all of the United States, and Joe worked at one of the most reputable companies in the world, as did I. We ate delicious food at every meal; we could even eat out at a restaurant for every meal if we wanted, and we often did.

We drove nice cars—as a matter of fact, Joe often had two cars of his own, while I had one. We went shopping for nice clothes and shoes all the time. We had so much excess, we literally had several trash bags of "unwanted" clothes and shoes that we donated each year. I even had a couple trash bags full of old purses that were donated as well. We went on two vacations each year, and all those things helped boost me temporarily, but there was no doubt that I felt empty inside, and I was earnestly seeking the Lord to help me figure out my life. I always prided myself in being happy and not letting the little things get to me. Well, things were most certainly bothering me—pretty much everything and everyone.

Undeserving

Why was I chosen to be part of Your kingdom?
Surely, there are far more who are deserving

You must have known how severely I needed You
How my heart was turning and becoming unnoticeable,
Rather than flesh and blood, it was tar and stone

I am the most undeserving of Christ,
The most deserving of Your wrath

It is truly only through Your grace and mercy
That I am forgiven and may live

How unfathomable that fact
And yet how incredible that truth

I love You Lord, and thank You.

It is June 2010, and it's been one year and three months since I first became pregnant. I have had two unsuccessful pregnancies so far. I went on living my life and going to work. Due to my anguish, I thought if I altered my work schedule to arrive between 5-5.30 a.m., I would be able to leave work sooner and spend more of my day outside of work. I'm asking the Lord to heal my heart and to allow me to become pregnant and have a healthy baby. Also during this time, Joe and I take many weekend trips to the beach or woods or parks, or anywhere for that matter.

I liked my life most when I was not at work nor at home. I have to say we did travel a lot, an aspect for which I am also grateful. We stayed with Brian, my brother, and Laura, my sister-in-law, quite a bit. They lived close to the beach so we were staying at their house all the time. They were so gracious, they provided us with our own bedroom, bathroom, fed us, took us out, and were so much fun to be around. If it wasn't for the weekend getaways and having Brian and Laura's house as a second home, I'm not sure I would have experienced any bit of enjoyment during those years.

I can't remember exactly when, but in September/October 2010, I miscarried again. This time, Joe and I decided to go through with Intrauterine Insemination (IUI) to help us become pregnant. It is a strange feeling to be so overcome with something you want that it is all you think about. It was on my mind all the

Chapter 6

time. I was reading articles and books and trying everything. Any woman or couple who has tried to become pregnant has tried the cough medicine, pineapple core, alkalizing foods, teas, lotions, temperature readings, and the list goes on and on. Since I was unable to get pregnant as quickly as I wanted, I thought getting professional assistance would make me happy. We tried IUI twice since the first one did not take, and it was a pretty stressful time.

All the printed materials say not to stress about it, but how do you not be stressed about it? Actually, people telling me not to stress about it and reading over and over again about how we shouldn't stress over it made me even more stressed. It is very stressful trying to get pregnant. It weighs down on you physically, spiritually, and emotionally. It controlled my life, and every month my period was a reminder of my failure to become pregnant, and on top of that, failure to keep the previous two pregnancies. I was fixated on getting pregnant, never mind that I hadn't been able to keep the previous ones.

On top of that stress is the tension of attempting to become pregnant via professional assistance. In my experience with IUI twice, I had to drive to Baltimore every day for a week or every other day for two weeks to get "checked" to see when I would be the most viable for a pregnancy. This meant I had to alter my work schedule each time, fight traffic on the way there and back, pay for parking each time, get "checked" out by different people, give myself injections, take pills or other forms of medication through various application methods to get my levels just so—and forget about the actual day of the procedure.

Looking back during those hectic and incredibly stressful times reminds me that "no one can serve two masters. Either you will hate the one and love the other, or you will be devoted to the one and despise the other. You cannot serve both God and money." (Matthew 6:24) Human beings are creatures who love to worship. Whether the object of our focus is money, job, car or trying to start a family, we all pour forth our efforts into something more than others. Not only was I worshipping money and job, I was also focusing on having a baby. I could not understand why God was not providing me with more. I had been praying for more promotions, more money, and for a baby. I did not understand back then that I was using God as a vending machine for whatever selection I wanted. I attended church, read the Bible, and prayed earnestly for things, and in turn, I wanted God to give me what I wanted. I was not looking to my Father in heaven as the one who provides for all my needs, I was looking to God to get me what I wanted, and give it to me right now.

We had an incredible strain on our marriage, and we were on the brink of divorce several times. At one point, we had an argument about something, I don't even remember the subject matter, but I was so angry, I picked up and drove two and a half hours to the beach to just get away. Ever since I was a child, one thing I absolutely loved was being at the beach. Of course it's fun and normal to be at the beach during the summer time, but I loved going during the fall and winter seasons as well—something about the intimacy of being alone with the vast ocean, sand, shells, birds, and smells that is missing when hordes of people are around.

I feel a calm that comes over me when I am at the beach. I've always said to Joe he was blessed to have a passion. He has a passion for cars, for fixing them and working on them. He is especially gifted with Volkswagens and European models, but he really has gifted hands for working on any model. It's nice to know you truly like something and are good at it. I have never known what I really liked to do. I'm not really passionate about any particular topic, but I know I do love being at the beach. I've always dreamed of having a beachfront home. We live about twenty-five minutes away from the beach now, and I hope we can move even closer to it one day.

So here I am at the beach and alone. I ended up spending the night at a hotel by myself. I did not know why I was so angry. I walked along the shoreline, looking out at the waves, taking in the sounds of the waves crashing, praying that God would take away my anger. I was angry with Joe and was praying I would have more patience with him. By God's grace, we are still married, and our marriage is healing and a lot better, not because of some program we followed, but because we decided we would personally develop a stronger relationship with our Father in heaven, which in turn has benefited and blessed our marriage.

We had tried IUI twice. The first time it didn't work. The second time, it worked, and I was pregnant. I remember receiving the phone call from the doctor's office. It was very early in the pregnancy. I was crying and praising God that we were pregnant. I had an acupuncture appointment in a few days, and I knew the retired pastor and his second wife would be thrilled for me. Upon arrival for my appointment, I couldn't contain myself, and I told them both I was pregnant. The wife and I started crying, and the pastor praised God. I had my normal acupuncture that afternoon, and I remember wondering whether or not I should go through with this appointment since I was pregnant. I thought it couldn't hurt since it probably helped me, so I ignored that voice and received the treatment anyway.

I had been going to the doctor's office twice a week to get my blood drawn to ensure my hcg levels were increasing, but by the second month, I had lost this baby too. I'm not saying that getting that acupuncture treatment was the reason why, I just wonder if I hadn't gone through with that last treatment, if I would have carried the baby to full term. Probably not, but that is something I used to wonder about. I was more confused than ever, even more unsure of how to feel, and just plain lost. Again, I carried all this inside, and I was still unable to describe my anguish to Joe. It was me, my pen and paper, God, and the Bible. The majority of my journal back then is filled with, "Why am I so angry?" or "Why am I so sad?" It's very lonely being sad and angry, and I could not find the words to express myself. I prayed so much during these years, and I praise the Lord that He never got tired of me—I most certainly was tired of myself.

There have been so many times I have ignored thoughts or nudges to do something. Whether the thought may be to let the person behind me in line go ahead of me, or pay for the coffee for the person behind me or to stop by a neighbor's house, they are all seemingly small things, but I make a decision to ignore that prompting. I found the more I listen and act upon them, the more I feel like I'm behaving like Jesus, which makes me happy. Thank You, Father, for being so patient with me, and for always loving me. After I lost the IUI baby is about the time I stopped getting the acupuncture treatment.

It was incredibly difficult for me at work. It was a struggle every morning for me to go to work, and I was not healthy, especially emotionally and mentally. I can remember attending meetings and thinking, "I could really give a crap about this." I really did not care, and yet others seemed so eager and engaged. I no longer cared about receiving the praise from my boss or ensuring I got credit on a project. It all seemed so unimportant. I blamed my managers and coworkers. I blamed everyone, and I was bitter. Not only was I disengaged, I didn't understand how some women can just become pregnant simply because they wanted to. Or how others were completely abusing their bodies with drugs and alcohol and didn't want babies, yet they were not only becoming pregnant, they were carrying these babies to full term. It is scary to think how much distress I was carrying around inside. I wonder how much others are carrying around and if they know they do not need to feel that way.

Chapter 6

Rusty passed out at Brian and Laura's house on one of our weekend getaways (June 2009) – First miscarriage occurred on March 16, 2009

Joe making me laugh about something. Hiking at C&O Canal, Maryland (Oct 2011)—had surgery in March/April 2011 for cyst removal

This was inside our resort in Riviera Maya. We had just arrived, and Brian was already cracking us up (May 2012)— had emergency surgery to remove burst ectopic in April 2012

Laura, bottom right, all engrossed in the Mayan pyramids ruin tour. Me and Brian hanging back as we're ready to move on to the next pyramid (May 2012)—had emergency surgery to remove burst ectopic in April 2012

Chapter 6

Joe praying with sun shining in our hotel room in OC. Praying that fetal pole will show up following week (April 2013)

Joe drinking Route 66 root beer while driving on Rte. 66 (May 2013) — miscarried in April 2013

Rte. 66 museum in Clinton, Oklahoma (May 2013)

Grand Canyon (May 2013) – part of our Rte. 66 road trip

Chapter 6

Ledge where we had lunch at Grand Canyon (May 2013)

Chapter 7

After my third loss, this last one from IUI, it was the fall of 2010, and my Rusty became sick. He was about nine years old; he had already become blind a year earlier. His organs just failed, and the vet asked if Rusty had access to contaminated river water or something. We didn't think so as we had to keep him on a leash, but it came time for Rusty to be put to sleep. The vet said Rusty could be transferred to a hospital where he could receive a blood transfusion, which would cost upward of $10,000, and there would be no guarantee of a full recovery. To say I was heartbroken does not justify my sadness.

This made me consider all the feelings we have and how God gave us all of them. There are different degrees of joy, love, and sadness. Each emotion in itself has its own scale. It's different to feel happy because you are eating the best pizza in the world, compared to being as content as when vacationing on some beautiful island. We all know the different aspects of love—loving a song to a family member to loving a car or spouse, those are all nice emotions to experience as well. But when you talk about the different components of sadness, it is a real testing of yourself as a person. For every different type of sadness you go through, who you become afterward manifests in different ways depending upon the sadness you went through.

For example, I think about some of the sadness I went

through growing up in a less than favorable environment. I went through that up until my early twenties, and as a result, I came out feeling so unsure of my feelings all the time, I didn't know if they were right or wrong. I did not know how to connect with people without alcohol for a very long time. I used to blame my parents, but they did the best they could, and I am thankful for them. They taught us how to work hard and that regardless of color, or lack of education, or the inability to communicate, you can achieve anything you want. It must have been difficult leaving their home country with four children in tow, unable to speak a foreign language, all in hopes of providing a better life for their kids, which they did.

The sadness I went through when my grandmother died was also different. She was old, and she had been saying to us for years how she would be gone any day now. I was certainly sad and experienced regret, but afterward, I came out neutral. That event didn't really change me much for better or worse, a little better probably, but that was temporary. The sadness I felt for years after multiple miscarriages has most certainly changed me for the better. Going through that was horrendous, but I thank God He got me through it, and I'm so grateful for the inner peace I now have. But the sadness I felt when we lost Rusty frayed what was remaining of my heart and soul.

Even though he was an animal and our pet dog, I really did love him. We spent nine years of our lives together, and he was such a good boy, the best one, I would argue. I don't know how to explain that type of gut-wrenching sorrow. I know there are different degrees to sadness, and the type I felt after losing Rusty has to be one of the most painful. I would imagine there would only be a few other instances where a deeper sadness would qualify for me. Our Father in heaven is love, and He is perfect love. He loves us sinners so much he experienced the worst sadness of all by sending His son, Jesus, to earth. Jesus loved His father so much that He went through with it. Jesus loved us so much that He died on the cross for our sins so we would not have to experience the punishment we deserve and now can have eternal life.

We cannot fathom that depth of love nor that degree of sorrow. I believe there are no human words that can appropriately describe such love and anguish. As you know, I loved my Rusty, and I would not have given him up to take the punishment for someone else, and again, he was my dog. God loves us so much, He sent His son to die for us. I don't know why You love me so much, Father, but thank You so much! The more you love, the more love you feel. You come to grasp that God's love for us is immeasurable. His love for us was displayed on the cross. Thank You, Jesus.

After we received word that I had lost the IUI baby, Joe and I decided to pray and fast. We fasted lunch every day for two weeks and prayed for healing and recovery. After our two week lunch fast, Rusty died. He was the best boy, and I'll always miss him. Both Joe and I were absolutely torn over the loss. We walked down the street with his leash just so I could feel closer to him. I was crying my heart out. I often dream that I'll be in heaven, and Rusty will be there with us, along with our babies.

Rusty has visited me several times in my dreams at night; he's beautiful, healthy, playing, and he's not blind. I can't wait to see him and play with him again. He opened a part of my heart I didn't know existed. He expanded my knowledge of love and allowed me to experience a different aspect of love. I feel God placed him in our lives to teach us about His immeasurable love. Love also has so many different facets, and with Rusty, I was able to feel a type of love I would not have otherwise experienced. I felt closer to God as I was able to experience another type of love, and since God is love, I felt another beautiful element of Him.

The day Rusty passed away, it was raining, a torrential downpour and thunder. It seemed as if God was showing the immense sorrow I felt physically through the storm, and somehow, that rain comforted me. The fact that everyone else in town was being inconvenienced by the storm and had to slow

Chapter 7

down seemed appropriate. As I think back on that now, I still can't help but shake my head; it really was crazy. We had just gone through another miscarriage, we fasted and prayed, Rusty had died, it is raining buckets, and guess what happens next? We get a flat tire.

At that point, I felt like God was playing a trick on us, as if to say, *Why are you taking things so seriously?* And boy, was I; I was very serious, gravely serious, about everything. It was difficult to find joy, let alone humor. Just when I thought things couldn't get any worse, we get a flat tire, and that's when I started laughing. I said, "Lord, you are just too much." I felt like I was in one of those movies where the main character is falling apart, and anything that could possibly go wrong has, and just when you think there's nothing else that could top what just happened, something does. That's when you throw up your hands and say, that's it, okay, I'm done. I was crying because of Rusty and everything else that had happened, and for some reason, I started laughing then too.

If any of our neighbors were watching us, they probably thought we were losing it. Here we are walking around with a leash and no dog, all-out crying, tears streaming down uncontrollably, and when we walk to our car, we realize we have a flat tire. When you're that numb, not much can shake you out of it. Yet, here I am, crying, and then I start guffawing at the same time, as I leaned up against our car. This wasn't the last time I would feel opposite emotions at the same time.

After the loss of this pregnancy and then Rusty passing away, I started developing a fear that Joe would die soon too. I kept thinking of horrible scenarios whenever he would step out of the house. I took my fears to the Lord in prayer, but it would actually make me so upset I would break down in tears because I felt as if he had already passed away. Fear of the unknown is a disease all of its own. It spreads and grows relatively rapidly based upon how much it is fed. The fear of all the potential negative outcomes has an appetite that is never satisfied. There is not one topic that fear cannot victimize and snatch up to exploit. It is crippling and leaves you in a state of "what ifs" to the point where fear rules over your life.

However, I believe the Lord knew this was too much for me at this point in my life and my fears were overcome within several months. Again, I took my fears earnestly to the Lord in prayer, had friends praying for me as well, and when I finally shared with Joe my fears, he was very understanding. Joe said the best thing that can happen to Christians is to die, to be eternally with our heavenly Father and that I should be happy for him. He also said if he were to die soon, he would be in heaven with Rusty and our babies and that they would all be waiting for me to join the party. Through praying, sharing my fears with Joe and friends, their prayers, and trusting in an exquisite after life, fear lost its grip on me, and I soared into the arms of our Lord and that tyrant has not been fed since. Thank You, Jesus.

By this time, I had been to several OBs, gone to nationally recognized infertility specialists, acupuncturists, read numerous books and articles, and honestly, I was plain exhausted, just drained of trying—trying to get pregnant, trying to be happy, trying to understand why I was having such an inner struggle with work, trying to understand why others are so happy. What perplexed me the most was when I would run into a non-Christian who was happy. I didn't understand how they could be happy at all. They knew about Jesus, yet did not believe in heaven or that He is the Christ. Here I am, a Christian, knowing I will go to heaven, but so sad. Nothing made sense to me.

Several months after the loss from the IUI, they found a large cyst on my left ovary. They said typically cysts come and go throughout the menstrual cycle, but this one kept hanging on. It was large enough they needed to surgically remove it. It was March/April of 2011 now, and I was undergoing my first surgery. They said it was the size of a grapefruit on my ovary. They would do everything they could to keep my left ovary intact.

They went in laparoscopically, and I thought my days of miscarriages were behind me. I didn't understand why I kept

Chapter 7

losing my babies, but at least now I could blame it on something. Whether the cyst was the true culprit or not, that's where I placed my blame. I felt very uncomfortable for a while due to the gases they used to inflate my belly for the surgery. I had remarkable bruising all over my stomach for several weeks as well. The doctor was able to save my left ovary and rather than removing the entire cyst, left a small remnant of it so he did not have to remove my ovary.

This is about the time I read about how many fake ingredients and hormones are used in conventional foods. I was completely ignorant in thinking as long as I had a grilled chicken salad from a fast-food restaurant, I was being healthy. Little did I know I was ingesting chemicals, hormones, antibiotics, and overall fake and unhealthy foods. I changed our diet to eat organic as much as possible. We discovered Whole Foods market, and I instantly fell in love with that place.

We were very grateful we had the opportunity to eat organic foods, and I was slowly starting to cook more. I was never very domesticated. Growing up, I hung out with my two brothers, and I was more interested in playing outside than cooking or doing laundry. Thankfully, Joe did not hold it against me, and wouldn't you know it, when we first met, he was a chef. He would bring me delicious food, and when we first got married, he did the laundry. As an adult, I was used to dropping off my laundry at the Laundromat, where they would wash and fold my clothes and have them wrapped up for me to pick up. So with organic food came some domesticating. I felt better psychologically knowing we were eating healthy organic food.

A couple of months after the surgery, I was writing less and less and getting more and more acclimated back to life. Growing up, I loved being around a lot of people, and I loved going to parties. There was something about going out or going to a party and just having a good time that really drew me. I always had a lot of companions. Looking back, I see they were not really friends, just acquaintances you see at the same gatherings and joked around with. Back then, it was fun to make fun of someone, especially when we were drunk or high, or brag about what you have or what you've done. Since 2003, it had been just me, Joe and Rusty, other than family. I had a few friends from church and work, but mostly, it was the three of us.

During that year from spring of 2011 to spring of 2012, Joe and I spent a lot of time outside, either hiking, walking, biking, going to the beach or going on vacation. Being away from our house or work was the only time I felt an ounce of joy returning back to myself. I know people like Fridays since they have weekends off, but it was more than that for me. I found myself taking off Fridays or Mondays whenever I could, as when I was not at work, I could feel layers of happiness growing inside me. I literally, with all my being, did not like work. It affected me physically and emotionally. I became someone at work that I am embarrassed to admit I was.

It was like Dr. Jekyll and Mr. Hyde when I was at work. I was mean, irritated, grumpy, the total opposite of who I wanted to be. When we were away for the weekend or on vacation, that was the person I liked being, focusing on Jesus, finding contentment at just being outside or enjoying the weather. I spent the next year blaming everyone at work for why I could not get myself to care about work. I came to dislike our house as well.

I thought getting new furniture, rearranging, and getting some new plants would help. It did a little bit, but I was never really comfortable in that house. We moved into that house in December 2007, and ever since we left in June 2013, I just never felt like it was home. It was a very nice place, more room than we needed, in a highly sought after neighborhood, and I had this feeling it was very temporary. I did not want to get comfortable, or could get comfortable. I was feeling even more restless in that house with Rusty gone, and I just felt anxious.

That, too, was ignored. I kept trudging along. I kept on feeling disinterested at work, confused about the losses, wondering why Joe and I couldn't get along, all while faithfully attending church,

Chapter 7

reading the Bible, and praying. It amazes me how your body, mind, and spirit tell you what it likes and does not like, yet we choose to ignore them. As a young child and growing up into adulthood, I was taught to work and make a lot of money. You are supposed to make a lot of money, because when you make a lot of money, that is how you become happy. Again, feeling contradicting emotions, I continued working because earning a good salary is eventually supposed to bring happiness.

Don't get me wrong, I coveted going away on weekends, on our many vacations to Bermuda, Bahamas, all throughout the Caribbean, traveling all over the states and to Mexico. We went on a cruise and to the Outer Banks each year. We took road trips to Canada, New England, and to neighboring states. I'm so thankful for all the blessings and opportunity to travel and having wonderful memories. Again, even with all this, I could not fool myself and deny that something inside of me was missing. I was aware of what we had, appreciative of it all, thanked the Lord for his many blessings every day. I was very confused as I knew I should be happier.

Chapter 8

It's been almost a year since my surgery, and I am trying to get by in life. I have friends praying for me, and I am settling in and forcing myself to accept that this is my life. It is now April 2012, and I started getting excruciating sharp pains in my stomach. I didn't know what was going on, but I was in immense physical pain.

The following is the actual e-mail I wrote to my friends in April 2012:

Hi Ladies,
My sleep pattern is off due to the meds, so I figured I'd take this time to explain what happened. I'm still processing it myself, and I think would help me to write it down as well.

It started last Monday/23rd when I was in class. Actually, I had experienced sharp pains a few days prior to that Monday, so I went to my primary, had blood work and ultrasound, she thought it was GI issues and ruptured cyst, a day later pains subsided. Then I experienced pains again last Sunday at church. As soon as service started I walked to the ladies room and was hunched over in a stall from the pain. It had subsided enough around offering time so I grabbed Joe and we went home.

Chapter 8

[From the start of service to the offering time is about 20 minutes, so I was in the ladies room stall doubled over from the sharp pains in my stomach during that time. The pains subsided enough for me to walk back into service and grab Joe so we could go home].

I wasn't feeling 100%, but well enough to sit in class for a week [I was scheduled to be in training for work this week]. *It was around 10.15a Monday when I started getting the pains again, I barely made it to the ladies room when I doubled over from the pain. It was so painful I broke out into an all body sweat and literally had sweat dripping off of me. I had never experienced that before. I laid there for over an hour waiting for someone to come in. No woman, no cleaning staff, no one until 11.30 when classes broke for lunch. Someone finally came in, she was nice enough to get my things from the classroom, then I drove myself to the ER as pain had subsided enough for me to drive.*

[Some lady saw me doubled over on the ladies room floor and said she was running to the front desk so they could call 911. At that time, the sharpness and pains had subsided enough where I could actually stand up. Mind you, I had been sweating from the physical pain, and until she showed up, I was not able to get myself up. I pleaded with her not to call 911 and asked that she grab my things from the classroom. I don't know what her name was, but if you are reading this, thank you.
When I got to my car, I called Joe and explained what had happened as he was at work. He was leaving work to meet me at the hospital].

Joe met me there and we waited a couple of hours before getting a room. [My pain level had decreased, but I was still in pain]. *They did ultrasound and blood work and hcg showed I was very early in a pregnancy. They wanted me to stay for at least another 2 days to do blood work and ultrasound each day. Pain had again mellowed and I did not want to stay there just for those tests, so I promised to get those tests done on my own from my obgyn. So they released me and allowed me to go home.*

I went to obgyn on Tue, had both tests done and results would be in Wed. He told me to come back Thu to repeat the tests. I came back Thu, did both tests again and again nothing concrete on ultrasound, but hcg levels steadily increasing. I hadn't been back to class and hadn't gone into work Tue or Wed, just wasn't feeling well overall. Went into work late Thu after my appt, and left work after several hours cuz I started feeling poorly overall again.

[During this time, I had a dull and achy crampy pain, but not like the spontaneous sweat dripping pain I experienced a few days earlier].

Routine Thu evening, went to bed, around 11.30p woke Joe as pains came back. [I was lying in bed when the screaming sharp pain hit me again in my stomach. I immediately woke Joe and said, "Something is wrong"]. *He called my obgyn, was told to give me 3 advils, 45 min later, I'm in excruciating pain.* [I am in so much pain I cannot move. I can't roll over to my side, let alone try to get out of bed. I had brief moments of relief when the piercing pain would subside, so Joe put a shirt and pants over my pajamas and we left].

We go back to ER around 1a.m., and I thought they saw me right away cuz I was a returning customer, but my symptoms were bad enough to get me in right away. Another blood test and a long ultrasound. This time they saw it in my left tube. [Mind you, I am in pain, they conducted the longest ultrasound to try to determine what was going on; in the meantime I was wrenching from the pain and bleeding].

They told me they had to perform surgery right away and that I couldn't leave the hospital as I wanted to go home and think about what to do, talk to my obgyn, but they said, that has to come out either laparoscopic or

Chapter 8

bigger incision, one way or another it was coming out. [At this point, I am dazed from being in pain, trying to compute that I am pregnant, all while they are telling me I am in danger.

Joe was incredibly stressed out because he didn't know what was going on. I was in a lot of pain, and the staff is saying I'm in danger, and then Joe starts throwing up from the stress. He's running to the bathroom, I'm confused, still in pain, wondering if this is my last day on earth.

The next thing I know, I'm on a bed being rolled down the hospital hallways to the operating room].

I was in a daze from meds, feeling beat from test after test, tired of being in pain, that when they were rolling me down the hallways, it hit me that I was getting surgery again, and I broke down in tears at that point. [I did not cry when I was in excruciating pain, it was past tears. The pain prevented me from doing anything, all I could do was sweat]. *They had to stop on the way there, call the anesthesiologist to sedate me before the actual sedation for the surgery.*

[I remember lying on the hospital bed, they are rolling me down the hallways to the OR. I started crying uncontrollably, and then they just stop in the middle of hall and push my bed to one side of the hall. The anesthesiologist is describing what will happen, but it just sounds like words. The words being formed are familiar, but they are not registering. As I lie there crying, someone walks Joe away from my hospital bed, and the last thing I remember is looking at Joe and he's walking backward down the hall looking at me with someone pulling at his arm].

I woke up, they told me they removed the ectopic pregnancy, it had ruptured, and they had to remove the damaged section of my left tube (theory is lingering scar tissue from last year's surgery blocked it?). It didn't hit me, still heavily medicated, I was thinking it wasn't a big deal. They discharge me Friday night around 9.30p.

I've been on some strong meds, and I think has shielded me from the events that occurred. I just stopped taking the one narcotic, and I can tell I'm starting to get more sad as the haziness is wearing off. They say I'm fortunate to have gotten the surgery when I did. It could've been a lot worse. I guess I'm blessed? If this is what being blessed means, I guess I am. We have a trip booked for Rivera Maya May 12, and I'll find out next Tue if I'm cleared to go. I'm thankful this didn't happen down there, I'm glad I have 1 good tube remaining. I'm grateful for Joe.

Thank you for praying for us, although I don't know what to pray for myself. Do I dare hope so fearlessly and request that I don't experience another loss? Is that my plight, my thorn, in my life? Am I supposed to say that God's grace is sufficient for me? Perhaps I'm being broken down until that is the only thing I say and believe. Am I strong enough to undergo such polishing? Not by myself.

Whatever the purpose, it is beyond my grasp, outside my understanding. Help me, Lord, to see, overcome, to be refined, and not defined, by these sufferings.
Yes, indeed, Father—Your grace is sufficient for me.

Su

What the heck is going on? Is this really happening to me? I must be in a bad nightmare that I need to wake up from. At this point, I am completely fed up. I hate our home, there are too many bad memories here, I hate my job, I hate my life. What is going on, Lord? Are you there? I feel trapped and helpless.

I am recovering at home and wondering if we'll be able to go on our trip. We had already paid. We were planning to go with Brian and Laura. I am angry, sad, wondering why I'm alive. I think that being in heaven would be a much better place and that living on earth is too painful. I keep asking the Lord why He didn't take me, and I start getting agitated that He didn't take me

Chapter 8

to heaven. At this point, I'm praying the doctor would clear me for Mexico as I really want to get away.

I continue praying, reading, and wondering for the next several weeks. Thankfully, I'm cleared for Riviera Maya, and I'm recovering well. It's strange, the year prior they removed my cyst, and they left a few scars, the incision points in my belly button, and a couple on my lower belly. To remove the burst ectopic, they went in the same incision points a year later. I was glad that I didn't have to get two different sets of scars.

During the next couple of weeks while I am recovering, I experience healing on different planes. When I first get home, I am shockingly all right, but I am on some strong medication too. I like feeling like this, nothing really bothering me. After about a week, I tried a few days without the medicine to see how I would feel. I was very sensitive, fragile and confused. The meds work really well and shielded me from my own feelings. I can see why some people get hooked; if you want to stop feeling badly, take some of these pills, and you know what? They work. It's as if they put another layer or shield around you, so that not only do other people not bother you, you don't feel the sadness within yourself.

Through the Holy Spirit working in me, somehow I decided to stop taking the pills. I wanted to take one every day, just to take the edge off, but through it all, Jesus sat next to me. While I wholeheartedly wanted to feel numb and to keep taking the medicine, the only spark of hope I clung to was that I wanted to be truly healed by God. Again, I had been struggling for years now for peace and joy, and I only wanted it from Jesus. It's not that it was being withheld from me, not at all, it was there all along, I was just so confused in trying to understand I did not need anything else but Jesus. I was trying to find my happiness in money, clothes, vacations, babies, and yeah, it was cool that I was a Christian too. Like Joe says, I'm such a knucklehead sometimes.

Joe was extremely busy with work, but we would spend a few hours together each night. He must have been so exhausted during that time. He was going through a difficult time at work, and here I am, I can't even keep our babies, have two surgeries two years in a row, and he comes home to a confused wife. One week after I got home from the hospital, the next Friday night, he talked me into going for a drive. It was the first time I'd been out of the house since I got home, and when we pulled out of our street, I started bawling my eyes out in the car.

It was a beautiful night so Joe kept driving us around. I'm crying, and he gently pats my knee as I sit there sobbing. While my world had paused, the rest of the world went right on living. After an hour of driving, we pull up to Cold Stone Creamery, and he buys me the most delicious ice cream I have ever had. It made me feel better, and I stopped crying. We drove around a little more, and it was normal for a little bit. When we were heading back home, I started getting a little nervous as I didn't want to go back home. I wanted to stay in the car and keep on driving around.

That's how I started getting out of the house. Joe started driving around, and I really liked watching the fields pass by, pondering how far the clouds had traveled, wondering where the birds were going, and it was a real treat to see possums, groundhogs, deer, and falcons. I especially liked it at night when we had a clear view of the moon. On a couple of Saturdays, and Sundays after church, if it was a gorgeous day, we would drive out to the country or some new place, and I would absolutely love it! I still cried in the car, but it was becoming less and less frequent. We would reminisce about funny things that happened in the past or talk about a stupid movie, and I started laughing too.

A few weeks later and with the doctor's blessing, Brian, Laura, Joe and I were off to Mexico. It was May 12, 2012, and we were in Riviera Maya. It's an hour south of Cancun, and Joe and I have been a couple of times already, but this was the first time we'd gone with Brian and Laura. We were staying in a beautiful resort, the weather was beautiful, and the water was perfect. Our rooms were next to one another, and we had a full week ahead of relaxation and fun. I was so thankful I was able to recover in such a beautiful place. Plus, we always have a great time with Brian and Laura, so it was a very happy time. We booked several excursions and had a wonderful time meeting a lot of new people.

One of the excursions was to a big theme park with several activities in one location. There was a 4x4 Jeep jungle drive, hand-paddle kayaking (which is incredibly tiring), swimming in caves and lagoons, sightseeing, and zip lining. Joe and I had been zip lining many times before so we were excited about this stop. There were eight or nine stops, and with each leg, the line was longer and higher. A couple of them were equipped for tandem zips, and it was just a great fun-filled day. I would get teary-eyed throughout the day as I was so grateful to be where I was and that I was well enough to fully enjoy the moments. God is so good.

On our zip lining part of the excursion, we were having a blast. The last zip line was the tallest and longest, which allowed for dual zips because of that. Joe and I were next in line, and we were getting prepped by the line operator. They checked the gear, ensured we were hooked onto the line securely, and showed us how to hold onto each other so we can zip together. During that "check and instruction" phase, the operator motioned for me to step up closer to the edge. As I edged closer and closer to the drop off, the momentum of walking to the edge of the cliff, along with the steep sloping off of the edge, I actually lost my footing and started launching off the line by myself. I did not know if I was already hooked onto the line when a strong wind took me over the edge, and I heard the operator literally scream profanity as I looked back in complete fright.

Trust me, when you are that high up on a cliff and the line operator belts blasphemy as you soar away, that is not a good feeling. I did not immediately fall to the ground as I thought I would; I appeared to be hooked on to the line, and when I looked back, Joe looked mortified and the operator had his arm extended and hand outstretched trying to reach for me. At this point I was zipping away, and I was terrified. I stared at the harness and hardware to see if I could tell when I would start falling. I contemplated grabbing the line with my hands, but I realized that isn't a good idea. I kept my eye on the line and where my line was attached and thought, "If it looks like my hardware will come loose, then I'll grab the line."

I thought I was going to die. I prayed, "Lord, please let me go quickly." My visit to the emergency room a month earlier started playing in my mind, and I thought I had lived through that episode because I was supposed to die on our vacation, not in a hospital. As I opened my eyes, I saw that I was approaching an open pit below me with a live cheetah pacing back and forth waiting for me to drop from heaven. No exaggeration, a section of the zip line is above a cheetah pit. The next thought that came to mind is, "Okay, I won't go quickly because that cheetah is going to eat me for lunch."

For some reason, I hadn't fallen off the zip line yet. I could now see the end of the line. Only, I stopped before I reached the end, just beyond the cheetah pit, because there wasn't enough weight on the line. So now, I was dangling at the highest zip line at the park, wondering when I'd fall, how many bones I'd break when I did, and curious as to how quickly the cheetah would leap out of his pit to feast on me. At this point, I saw that the operator at the end of the line needed to come out manually, hand over hand over the line, to get me. I was surprised to see he did reach me. We were able to reach the end of the line safely, and I chuckled inwardly as I thought on how funny God is.

I was in a bit of a shock when Joe arrived a few moments later, freaking out asking if I'm okay. He thought I was going to fall as well, as did Brian and Laura. Joe said he was scared to death I was going to fall. While he didn't say so until we were back home, Joe said he was scared for the remainder of our vacation as he couldn't shake that feeling that I was going to fall for the rest of the trip. A few moments later, Brian and Laura arrived in tandem, asking what happened. Brian and Laura were describing how that last jump was really scary to launch off of because it was so high up. It turns out I was hooked onto the line, but the operator didn't realize I had already been hooked and plus, this was a tandem jump, so I shouldn't have launched off by myself. That was my second brush with death in a span of a little over one month, and I started feeling like I needed to live for some reason. The four of us still talk about that today, and we laugh about it now, but Joe says it still scares him to think about it.

Chapter 9

We had the most wonderful time. I am so thankful for that trip. Not only was I completely healed physically to wholly enjoy every aspect of our vacation, it was a great place to heal emotionally and mentally. At the end of May 2012, we celebrated our nine year anniversary. Joe and I were slowly rededicating our marriage to the Lord. We've had so many arguments, hurts, and just plain bad times that we sincerely want God to heal us individually and as a couple. Even after all the losses, I feel that I still want to get pregnant and start a family. Am I insane? Why can't I let go of the fact that we are not meant to have children? When will I learn that this is not for us?

Even after everything I've been through, I'm frustrated that I can't let go of the idea of having children. Historically, when I would set my mind to do something, I work hard at it and, *voila*, it's achieved. It was really bothering me. It was a personal under-achievement that I was working extremely hard at starting a family, and for some reason, I kept losing the babies. The problem wasn't that I was not getting pregnant, the problem was that I, me personally, cannot seem to house the little ones, which is a painful, jarring, slap in the face that I am personally responsible for in not providing a family for us. It was a real ego deflator, so I thought I would be okay if I just made more money. I was more concerned about what people

Chapter 9

must be thinking of me than what I should be doing to make myself healthier and happier.

I started finding another reason to be upset with Joe as I wanted to move out of our house, but Joe thought we should wait. I'm mad at myself and everyone as I am under so much stress at work, I just can't seem to find my stride, my rhythm, and my life isn't going the way I planned. I blame work and our house for my sadness. Also, I'm feeling more like a curse to others. I'm embarrassed to tell people I'm praying for them, as look at where it has gotten me. I know my non-Christian friends and family members are asking "Where is your God through all this?" I keep on believing, praying, reading, and crying. Even though I have a hurricane of emotions storming inside of me, mostly anger, bitterness, and sadness and a few occasions of relief sprinkled in when we go away, I know something inside me tells me to keep holding on to God's promises, that this is not the end, that there is so much more to my life.

Waiting is a difficult discipline to appreciate. I was not a good waiter, even for the tiniest of things. I did not like waiting in line at the store and was especially annoyed at being placed on hold over the phone. In the environment I used to live in, it's typical to cut someone off while driving in traffic just to be one or two cars ahead. I would literally get so upset waiting in a store or at the doctor's office, I would just walk out. I would inconvenience myself and go to the store, again, or take off work again to go back to the doctor and make sure I complained about know how long I had to wait the first time.

That's the culture we live in today; it's all about what is next. What I am doing now, in the present, is not good enough. I want what I think I should have and right now. No waiting, I worked hard for everything I had, no one gave anything to me. Since I worked hard for everything in my life, I deserved to get what I wanted. However, God is so good; He is so patient and loving with me. God was teaching me to stay in the present with Him, to overcome my past and to hope for the future, but in the meantime, to simply enjoy now. "Now" backward is "won," and I'm learning that for me, I've won when I'm in the now with Christ. Whether I'm waiting in traffic, doing the dishes, walking along the beach or reading my Bible, as long as I stay in the present and thank Jesus for what He has done for me, I enjoy whatever it is I am doing.

Have you ever run into some folks who are stuck in some era? We may think some people are stuck in the seventies, eighties or nineties by their hairstyle or clothes. But for others, it goes deeper than that; some cannot get past a hurt or an event in their life. That was the image that haunted me as I was in the process of getting better. I knew where I wanted to be, but I kept getting derailed over little things, which would frustrate me. I felt I was stuck by my past, by my losses, by my frustrated life, and I did not know how to get past all my crap and live the life I so badly wanted. But I kept praying, reading Scripture, and crying out to God. I wanted Him alone to make me better as I had tried everything I could think of and it wasn't getting me anywhere but bitter.

It's November 2012. I feel like I want to try again for a baby. Yes, I know, I have utterly lost it. We heard about an actual formerly trained acupuncturist. He's a doctor who has been practicing professionally for decades. I started seeing this second acupuncturist in hopes of getting pregnant and keeping the baby this time. He didn't believe in acupuncture for infertility; instead he prescribed herbal teas. I drank his concoction two times a day for twenty-five days and still no pregnancy after a couple of months. He said since I had experienced multiple miscarriages, I had a weak womb and that I should not run or walk too much. He also said I might need a second batch of his special fertility brew, but I thought it was too expensive at $425, so I declined. Both acupuncturists believed I had a weak womb and was the culprit behind my losses. They said I had just enough energy to support myself and that I was not strong enough nor had the resources to support a baby in my womb. I'm not sure what to think or believe, but I know no one is able to help me.

Chapter 9

Here we are, I have experienced numerous losses, I am without a left tube and only have a viable right tube working. Wouldn't it be funny if after all this, I become pregnant? This would truly be a miracle and God's hand working. I continue to cling to God's word and pray, yet still feel unhappy and irritated. How do I become happy with what I have? What are my hobbies, my passion? I have no idea. I'm trying to figure out what I like by trying different things, and while they all seem enjoyable enough, it really wouldn't bother me if I stopped doing any of them.

After trying knitting, cross-stitching, taking keyboard and guitar lessons, running, tennis, cooking, interior decorating, organizing, baking, online games, puzzles, volunteering, teaching, babysitting, and I don't know, probably a dozen other things, I realize what I enjoy the most is the beach, hiking, writing, traveling, and hanging out with Joe. After thirty-eight years of being on this earth, those are the things I truly enjoy. Of course, without spending time in prayer, reading the Bible, and fellowshipping with other believers, those interests would not be as enjoyable. For me, having a personal relationship with my Father in heaven, through Jesus Christ, makes everything sweeter and more fun. After the years of partying, drinking, drugs, material things, and climbing the corporate ladder, those things I thought made me happy are just chasing after the wind. It has no real meaning; therefore cannot offer the true joy and peace that comes from knowing the Lord.

I've also come to realize that working in a corporate office culture does not make me happy. What I have never understood since entering the corporate world over fourteen years ago is that hard work, solving problems, and making progress is secondary to office politics. In college and grad school, we are graded by how hard we study or understand a concept, or how well a paper was written. I achieved my grades through hard work, and I was the person on the group project ensuring everything was done and on time, even if I had to complete your part of the project. I like working hard, and I'm good at it. When there's a challenging project or issue at work, I like the sense of accomplishment from completing or resolving it. But, that's only a small fraction of how you are evaluated in the corporate world. The true measure of one's worth depends more on how well you can mingle with executives and play the "behind the scenes" games. I admit I was on that train and climbed my way up the ladder, only I really did not like myself at work. I was doing well at work and doing what we are supposed to do in achieving the American dream, only my life was far from a dream. Maybe I was living someone else's dream, but I certainly was not living mine.

As I contemplate now on that uneasiness and that internal voice of being unsettled, I believe it was the Holy Spirit leading me to leave the corporate world. Only, how could I? That would be insane! I worked my tail off to get where I was; now I am just supposed to leave the mainstream? Everyone I meet is impressed with where I work, the position I've climbed to, and plus, that goes against everything I have been taught growing up and in school. Rather than trusting the Holy Spirit's leading, I struggled with what was in front of me, the material world. I needed a nice car, pretty clothes—getting my hair done alone takes money, not to mention our organic diet, traveling or whatever cute knickknack I wanted. But, God is so good, when we decided to move closer to the beach, He provided a job for me right away at a big medical facility. However, again, I was feeling unsettled, but it's only about work this time, not for every other aspect about my life or marriage or having children, which is a big step forward.

I realized I need to make that enormous leap of faith and leave the medical facility. I'd been working there for a few months, and while I was very grateful that the Lord blessed me with that job, it was the only aspect of my life I felt unsettled about. My goal is to live wholly content, now, with Jesus, and if that means we don't have the money we are used to, so be it. Today, the Lord has blessed our marriage, has healed me physically and emotionally, brought us to a new life by the beach, and the one source of distress I have remaining is working in the corporate world.

Chapter 9

Even as I write this presently, I am hesitant about leaving, but Lord, I will. I will listen and follow, regardless of what I think makes sense or not. This makes no sense at all to anyone in the world; even some of my other Christian friends would think this careless, but Jesus, I keep my gaze on You, and the things of this world grow strangely dim. Thank You, Father, for not leaving me alone, for knowing what lies ahead for me and doing immeasurably more than all we ask or imagine (Ephesians 3:20).

It is December 2012. I had a vivid dream. In the dream, I walked into a big house where everything was a mess and in shambles. There was broken glass strewn about the floor, and the place was just littered with trash and clothes and debris. I realized Mom and Dad had had another fight. At that moment, I felt as I did as a child when they would fight—insecure, scared, angry, unprotected, all at the same time, simultaneously feeling all the negative feelings you could think of, even physically sick to my stomach. It's difficult to put into words how you feel as a child, or even as an adult, when something wrong happens, because there are many feelings, perhaps too many to name, so we just say, I don't know how to describe it.

After all the jagged emotions washed over me, I then became incredibly angry at my parents. This wave of burning anger just took over. It was the only emotion I was feeling. Next thing I know, we're at a lake or ocean, in front of a massive body of water and my mom was in a small canoe by herself, rowing away from me and the shoreline, just looking at me, as she rowed away using both paddles. Then I realized my dad was there too. I look away from my mom and see my dad to the left of me. He gently cups and pats me on the shoulder and starts walking away from me too. At that moment as I watched my dad walking away and I looked back at my mom rowing away, it hit me they were both going away to die. I was so sad, I started crying in my dream. I actually woke up crying.

As I sat up awake and crying, I realized I was holding on to so much anger toward them, I instantly felt foolish for holding on to it for all these years. I prayed that the Lord would help me to truly forgive them and love them. The next day I told Joe about the dream, and I started crying again. Not only did I explain my dream, but I also explained how utterly unhappy I was. How I wanted to move out of the house, and how I especially disliked where I worked. What he said next surprised me a little bit; he said he had never seen that side of me before. He had never really seen me crying in the twelve years he's known me.

Of course I cried after each loss and when Rusty died, but other than that, I haven't really cried in front of him. I cried in front of him when we would drive around before we left for Mexico, but I did the bulk of my crying in front of the Lord in prayer. I didn't realize it, but I had been shielding myself from him and everyone else. I realized God was healing my heart and soul when I opened up to Joe. That was my defense mechanism, keeping my feelings guarded and covered so that they could not be hurt. When Joe and I were dating and for several years after we got married, I felt very uncomfortable holding hands with him in public. I thought that exposed too much of my feelings, and I have always been careful in showing any emotion other than laughter. I would actually get very mad at Joe when he would try to hold my hand in public and slowly, very slowly, I was able to hold Joe's hand in public. Today, I'll reach for his hand when we're out in public. Joe says the next step is for me to kiss him in public, to which I say, "not gonna happen."

The Lord has done wonders in our marriage over the past year. He has healed both of us as Joe was hurting as well. He had gone through the roller coaster of emotions of thinking he would be a dad to no, never mind, he won't be a dad. Not just once or twice, but year after year for five years. He had to be there when I had two surgeries, two years in a row. He had to try to make me comfortable while working full time, trying to be happy for me, taking care of the household chores. Husbands cannot heal their wives, they can certainly assist in making their lives easier, but only Jesus could heal a hurt this deep, and thankfully, the Lord was not through with me yet. At a time when I thought my life was useless, meaningless, and, frankly, I did not see a reason to live, that's when He was just getting started.

After my vivid dream and my slow start in opening up to Joe, I continued to keep my tears and fears with the Lord through reading and prayer. It is now March 2013. Guess what? I'm pregnant. "I waited patiently for the Lord; he turned to me and heard my cry. He lifted me out of the slimy pit, out of the mud and mire, he set my feet on a rock and gave me a firm place to stand. He put a new song in my mouth, a hymn of praise to our God." (Psalm 40:1-3)

Chapter 10

I started a new journal and seriously considered ripping up and burning all my old journals up to this point. I wanted a new slate, a new story. I did not want to be reminded of everything I had been through so far and wanted no trace of evidence of my previous losses. It is March 25, 2013. I have an appointment with my doctor tomorrow for the first dating ultrasound. Things are looking up at work as well as I was able to find a part-time position. I'll be working twenty-five hours per week with my new work schedule, and I felt I was justifying going part time since that would help in working toward leaving the corporate world.

It seemed as if things may have been finally looking up for me. I was going part time. That should help me be less stressed out since I was pregnant. Around this time is when I started getting an inkling that I should keep my journals in case I wanted to write a book in the future. I quickly rolled my eyes at that notion as there was NO WAY I would ever share what I had been through. I was too embarrassed to confess that I was unable to keep my babies. I was too guarded with my feelings to open up to strangers about how bad I felt. I was just starting to open up to Joe about my feelings, and that had taken me over ten years. I did not want to be associated with such a messy and unsuccessful experience, so my intentions were to burn my journals so there would be zero chance of anyone ever discovering them.

Chapter 10

One month before I found out I was in pregnant, in February 2013, I filled out the prayer card at church asking the pastors and deacons to pray we would get pregnant. One unsuspecting day during that month, I was more unsettled than usual. I felt an incredible burden to pray. I actually felt heavy in my heart and soul, and nothing seemed to take away that weight away. I tried reading, taking a walk, and asked God why I felt so troubled. I was also fasting and praying earnestly for a pregnancy during this time. That day in prayer, I felt compelled to keep praying longer than usual. I had been praying and crying out to God in my room for an hour and a half. Joe had come home early from work that day, and he came upstairs to our bedroom to say hello. After he went back downstairs, I felt as if I wasn't finished praying yet. I still felt disconcerted so I went into my closet, closed the door, and really prayed. I poured out my heart and soul in there for over six hours. When I came out of the closet, I had no idea I had been in there that long.

I asked God to heal me from all my losses, from my past, from my bad choices, from the way I was living my life. I asked God to forgive me, for I knew I was not living my best life for Him, which perpetually fed into my dissatisfaction with myself. I thanked God for Jesus and what He had done for me and the world. I prayed through all of the hurts that came to mind, all the hurts I have caused, for the world, for sin, and I prayed I would get pregnant again. If I could get pregnant with just one working tube, I knew I could continue to hope for a family. I lifted up our marriage as we had such a long way to go. I earnestly asked the Lord to work in my life, and I prayed that I wanted to live my life for Jesus and for Him alone. After all that was said and done and I had not one more tear to shed, it had pretty much taken up my whole day.

It's a real place when you meet with God in prayer. It was just me and my cries to God. I wanted desperately to be pregnant again and just to be at peace. I have never spent so much time with the Lord in one sitting before. I poured out my all, and wouldn't you know it, a week later, I found out I was pregnant, again. I was so happy and feeling as if God was on my side. I wrote a letter to our church leadership and our friends to thank them for praying for me as well.

Admittedly, I was in shock and, while ecstatic and full of hope, fearful as well. There is an unnerving flurry of sensations when one is full of so many juxtaposing emotions. How can one be hopeful and fearful? Stressed and relieved? Full depth of high and low at once? How does one describe such vastness, the expansion of contrasting emotions? As I read Scripture and picture Jesus, beaten, broken, and torn on the cross, I can't help but describe it as "Amazing Beauty."

Amazing Beauty

Lord, did you know it would hurt this much?
The mission to overthrow sin's clutch

Then the promise of being reunited with the Father,
Becoming Lord and Savior

Did you experience fear and yet joy?
The torment to save the world from its ploy

Being separated from truth and love
Righteously timing the day of divine reunion

How long did it feel like to be separated from I AM
Were you longing yet wholly content

At such a stunning cost
The everlasting price has been paid

It's your amazing beauty
Holy essence, disfigured and bent

Chapter 10

Are your scars now just a story
Since you have entered your glory

You are my Paradise
But first, this life

I too have scars—physical scars on my stomach from both surgeries, spiritual scars as I continue on with this life, waiting for Jesus to take us home. Emotional scars as I heal and let go. This is my story, this is my song, praising my Savior, all the day long. I ended up miscarrying this pregnancy as well. Losing this one shocked even my doctor as he thought I would carry this one to full term. In the end, there's much speculation as to why I can't keep a pregnancy, but nothing concrete is known.

During one of the regular doctor visits, the sonogram showed no fetal pole. They asked me to come back in one week. If the fetal pole was not visible at the next visit, they said I would most likely miscarry. I was a wreck. We asked for prayers, and to get our minds off the situation, we went to the beach for the weekend. We stayed in one of the usual hotels we typically stay in and used that time to read the Bible and pray. The next morning, the bright sun was shining into our room so Joe opened the balcony door and let the light flood in. I lay in bed with my eyes closed, listening to the sound of the waves crashing, and when I opened my eyes, Joe was sitting by the balcony sliding glass doors, basking in the sun and praying. I thanked the Lord for Joe as I sat up and began praying as well.

The next week, we were in the doctor's office. He said the baby didn't have a heartbeat and had stopped growing. He said I would either miscarry naturally or they would surgically remove it. I went numb. I looked at Joe, looked at the doctor, back to Joe, and then back to the doctor. I finally said, "You're joking, right? You're playing a cruel joke." As I said it, I knew it was real. I was replaying what the doctor had said over and over again in my head as he continued speaking to us. Joe was upset and crying, but I just kept looking at him and the doctor as if I was in a dream. I felt like they were discussing something really bad, but I was a bystander witnessing it. Only I wasn't a bystander, I was the main topic, and the something really bad they were discussing involved me, again.

After several minutes of conversation, the doctor left us in the room. I didn't say a word. Joe was just looking at me to see how I would react. It was difficult for me to take it in, and while I was still trying to register that I would go through another miscarriage, the doctor walked back in the room and handed me some paperwork on a clipboard. I asked him what it was. He said he had just explained to Joe what all the documents were. He asked me to sign at the bottom of the forms, and I asked him what I was signing. He looked concerned as he turned to me and said they were the authorization papers to conduct the D&C if I hadn't lost the baby naturally in a day or two. As I sat looking at the clipboard, I thought it was a great invention. Someone needed some paper to write on, to keep it in place and with a sturdy backing; what a great idea.

The doctor started talking to Joe again, and I started reading the form. It spoke of the process, its risks, and that's when I started crying. The words went blurry and my tears dropped onto the paperwork. I couldn't believe I was losing this baby too. The next thing I knew, we were in the car driving home, and Joe was on the phone with our pastor. As I sat crying in the car and not knowing what to do, we ended up in our church parking lot. Joe said that Pastor Tim was available to pray with us. To tell you the truth, I don't remember much of that. I remember that Tim prayed for us, read us Scripture, and I just broke down in his office. I kept asking Tim to tell me what to do to get better. Do I fast for a month, should I paint a house, what was the process? What do I do? Pastor Tim, thank you for praying with us and for us.

Thankfully, I was in the transition of switching to part-time at work, and my new boss was incredibly understanding of my

Chapter 10

situation. While he did not come out and say it, it seemed as if he may have gone through a similar situation. I needed some time off, to say the least, and I wasn't sure when I would be ready to pick up and move on. I called him one afternoon to discuss a possible resignation, and he gave me some really good advice. He asked me to think about it for several more weeks. If I still felt compelled to leave the agency, he would accept my resignation then, but in the meantime, the position would be held for me. I was overwhelmed by the gesture. I started crying on the phone. I went from not crying in front of anybody to crying in front of everybody, even on the phone.

During this time, we went to the beach, of course. We stayed with Brian and Laura, of course, and I was trying to make sense of everything. In the past several years, nothing had worked out the way it was supposed to. You hear stories about someone going through really difficult things, and it's weird when that someone is you. When people tell bad experience stories about someone they know or what people are going through, I'm that person people refer to as "you think you have it bad, listen to what's happened to Su." I'm that person about whom everyone says, "Oh, that must be so tough." How in the world did I become that person? Lord, why am I that person?

Joe and I continued praying, reading together and fasting for healing and comfort. Joe was hurting over the loss of our babies, as well as over everything I had been through. He never made me feel like anything was my fault. He would only say, "God has a plan for us," and I would question him, "How do you know?" I was confused and couldn't understand why I was going through all this. We started talking about what we wanted to do. Joe felt we needed to get away. He needed a break from work as well. We threw around some ideas and settled on embarking on one of our bucket list items of things to do.

It is May 2013 and Joe and I have decided to go on a road trip. We have always wanted to take a road trip and drive across the US by way of Route 66. We dreamed of it often, but it was one of those pipe dreams, like backpacking across Europe for several weeks. It was a fantasy, way off in the distance, something we just talked about. Then we decided we would go for it. God's timing through all my losses was perfect. While I would have wanted nothing more than to have carried each pregnancy to full term, each one I lost happened at just the right time.

Typically, we have a trip booked in April or May, then again in December or January. Each miscarriage or surgery happened before our trips, just in time for me to be completely healed physically for our getaways. The trips afterward were even more appreciated as I continued healing emotionally, spiritually, and psychologically. While I was still sad inside, those trips helped me hang on to the beautiful things of this life, not only gorgeous beaches and having fun, but the real beauty that happens through love, patience, forgiveness, and healing.

I again asked Joe if we could move, and this time he agreed. After everything we had been through, I don't think there is much he would've said no to. He even agreed to take three weeks off of work so we could embark on our once-in-a-lifetime trip. This is about the time when the happy/sad scale started tipping favorably inside of me. Previously, I was mostly sad, with pockets of relief as we went away or I was engrossed in reading and praying. But I started feeling a slow shift, where I was gradually beginning to feel a peace grow inside of me, with pockets of sadness.

Before we left for our trip, I packed up a lot of our belongings, boxed up pretty much everything but the essentials, and put our house up for sale. In two weeks, I had the house completely ready for showings. I think that was one of the hardest things I have ever worked on. It made me think of how hard we work in order to win the approval of others, and on the opposite end of the spectrum, our Father in heaven accepts us as we are. Not only accepts, but knows all our darkest sins and somehow still love us; that is absolutely remarkable.

Working on the house, cleaning it, and sprucing it up for

Chapter 10

the showings helped me keep my mind off my circumstances. I was happy we were actually making plans to move and plus, I was looking forward to our drive across the country. Mind you, during this time, I continued reading the Bible and praying and pretty much every time I prayed, I cried. I was still healing not only from this last miscarriage, but healing from every hurt I had gone through. I was letting go, asking for forgiveness, and learning to forgive myself. It made me wonder about how miraculous our bodies truly are. I'm still alive, I'm healing, and I am able to produce unending tears. If you have ever cried for long periods of time, it really does make you wonder how the body can produce so much of the stuff.

It was time for us to leave on our trip. We were packed, the house was ready for showings, our mail was stopped, our niece had a key to check on the house and water the plants, and I was eager to get on the road. We packed our Honda Civic Hybrid with cases of water, a cooler full of snacks, and our luggage for the next three weeks. It is Sunday, May 12, 2013, Mother's Day, and we are leaving for our trip. It's funny that a year earlier, it was May 12, 2012, and we were leaving for Riviera Maya. That first day, we drove through West Virginia, Pennsylvania, back through West Virginia, and ended up staying the night in Ohio. I thought about God's sense of humor and how we started our trip on Mother's Day. It made me cry, but I ended the day with a smile.

As we left our house, street, city, county, and state, I felt more and more relieved. As the miles were compounding on top of one another, I was going toward a new life and leaving the old one behind. We reminisced about Rusty and how he had gone on numerous road trips with us. We spoke of other trips we wanted to take; for instance, how exciting it would be to finally tour Europe, going through Italy, Germany, France, and England. I spoke of going on African safaris and going down under, mate. This Route 66 road trip made those trips seem more attainable. Needless to say, I would inevitably get sad over my losses, and I cried openly as well.

One of the great aspects about taking road trips in the US are the rest stops. Some of them are very nice. What a great idea, to provide a safe break for people and their pets. We drove about seven or eight hours each day, sometimes only six, depending upon the nearby attractions or if we liked a certain town. We drove through many towns and had a great time in each. It was awesome driving on Route 66 and being able to see all the old splendor and attractions. We met quite a few international vacationers along the way as well. There was a group of bikers from Argentina, probably fifteen of them in biker gear, and all of them had beautiful bikes. They all flew up from Argentina and took a couple of weeks off away from their families and work to bike some of Route 66.

We would see them on the road and even stopped along some of the same attractions. There was a couple in a camper doing the same. We ran into a cute family with kids and grandparents, and we saw them at a few stops as well. It was a great time, and even being on the road, we would see not only cows and horses, but buffalo, foxes, falcons, beautiful skies, old railroad cars, and abandoned towns. It was a good reminder that most of America is not as populated and fast-paced as where we came from. I can't help but think how good Americans have it. We are so blessed as a nation and country.

I'm also thankful we were able to take a break, be completely out of our element, focus on new things, and heal. We stayed in a hotel each night with a pool and fitness center to get some exercise in since we were sitting in the car most of the day. Every evening and morning we read the Bible and prayed together. On Sundays we visited local churches in the town we were staying in. Sometimes I would cry when we were on the road, but the tears were for many different reasons. Of course I was upset as I thought about my losses, and how I would look forward to meeting them in heaven one day. But I also thought about the children who are hungry or unloved and how our Father in heaven must feel for them.

Chapter 10

I thought about family members and friends who do not understand God's love for them and how they may never be saved. I thought about how God allowed Joe and me to marry. Joe has this uncanny knack for loving me, even when I am irritated or just plain mean to him. His love for me reminds me of God's love for me, that no matter what, He loves me. During this time as I pray and cry, I cry because I'm healing, but I also cry for all the hurt in the world. It breaks my heart to think of how much we hurt our God by our sins, especially mine, and I am blown away as I come to grasp that I am already forgiven. As I learn to understand more of how great God is, I become overwhelmed and am often left speechless as there are no earthly words to righteously capture this divine love. Thank you, Holy Spirit, for interceding for me with groans that words cannot express (Romans 8:26). They are heavenly prayers for me that the Holy Spirit is offering to God. Wow, thank You, Jesus.

Chapter 11

While we were away, over two dozen people walked through during the open house. In a week and a half, our house sold. The story behind that is also unbelievable; God is so funny in how He works. Thank You, Lord, that our house sold so quickly and seamlessly in the end. Selling a home is incredibly stressful but we were able to be away on our trip of a lifetime. Don't get me wrong, I put in lot and lots of hours and hard work in two weeks to get the house prepared, but the Lord made it all work. Even though we had multiple issues to work through, our house was in divine hands, and the Lord made it all come together in the end. It's funny how, in retrospect, the Lord is so clearly working in our everyday lives, yet I was so focused on the things I thought were going wrong, I was too engrossed in looking down from my perspective, when I should have been looking up to appreciate God's perspective.

He was still teaching and reinforcing that He is in control, not us. I had to live by faith and trust Him completely and, wouldn't you know it, this transaction was done! Cash deal, no appraisal, no inspection, it was nothing but sold! Thank You, Jesus, for your patience with me. We had a wonderful time on our Route 66 road trip. We hiked a few mountains in Sedona, Arizona, and a good portion of the Grand Canyon. There were so many historical attractions and lots to do, we could probably write a book on that

Chapter 11

trip alone, but while we were in Arizona, we received word we had a buyer for our home.

Rather than taking a couple more days to drive to the end of Route 66 to California, we decided it was time to end our trip and drive back home. Retrospectively, what we should've done was rented a car and taken more time to drive all the way to the end, then flown back, but we spent several days trying to get back home so we could finalize the sale of our home. It was more stressful driving back home as we had an agenda. Originally, we were going to stop along different towns on the way home as well, but we bypassed all of them and drove straight home. By the way, we have to give a shout out to the rest stop in Texas. The location is perfect, the scenery is beautiful, and the facility itself rocks.

We're back home now from our trip. It's May 30, 2013. What a wonderful trip! I am refreshed and exhausted. We are so thankful that we were kept safe and just got home from a vacation that seemed like a distant, far away dream. When I first set foot in our house, I felt a little sad as I knew I had to come back down to my real life now that I was home. It was easier to be in the present being on the road and experiencing new adventures. But I did feel better, and knowing we were selling our house certainly helped as well.

We rented a townhouse from my other brother Kenny and Kristy, our sister-in-law. They had a house up the street from us, and they were nice enough to rent the place to us for a few months. Again, the Lord's timing is so perfect. Joe and I were going to rent an apartment until we decided where we would move, and during this time Kenny and Kristy purchased a new home. They were in the process of moving into their new home and were looking for renters for the home they just moved out of. Wouldn't you know it, we needed a place to rent and the Lord provided for us both.

I would be starting my new part-time position with the government in a few weeks. We still had to settle on our home, pack up the remaining items, move out, move in, and then unpack. I was so happy to move out of our home, there were so many bad memories, and like I said, I just never felt very comfortable there. When we moved into Kenny and Kristy's down the street, it felt even more temporary than ever. Joe and I knew we would not be there for long. We were praying about where to move to. We thought we would purchase a small condo for us to live in and a beach home for the weekend getaways.

We went away each weekend to look at homes near the beach. We would either make a day trip out of it or stay the weekend with Brian and Laura. One day as we were driving back home from one of our day trip visits, Joe saw a billboard that said something like "turn here for homes." We decided to check out that neighborhood. The usual process was that I would do immense amounts of research online on the neighborhood, proximity to the beach, traffic, etc., and if there were some homes that met the criteria we had set, we would drive to that neighborhood. If we liked the home and neighborhood, we called the agent to come meet us to show us around inside. After numerous visits to Maryland and Delaware area beaches, there wasn't anything that really stood out. Then Joe sees the billboard, and wouldn't you know it, that's the neighborhood we moved into. No research or legwork needed, God again provided for it all. The transaction was seamless, easy, and heaven sent. We rented from Kenny and Kristy for several months before moving out.

Because we loved the house and area so much, we decided to pick up and move our lives to Delaware. While we are still about twenty-five minutes from the beach, it is nice to know I can drive to the beach any time I want to. My dream is to one day live in a beachfront home, but until then, being half an hour away is an incredible blessing. We are surrounded by farm land and live near cows, horses, and donkeys. It was a bit strange at first as I could smell them whenever I walked outside, but now it's normal. The way of living is just my pace as there are no honking horns, no bumper-to-bumper traffic, and we have to drive twenty-five

Chapter 11

miles per hour on these roads until you hit the main roads. We sold everything in our home but our clothes; all the furniture we sold or donated. We came with our clothes, books, computers, and other miscellaneous things.

It's incredible, and sad, how much crap we accumulate, a lot of useless junk that is kept and kept and for what? Lord, help me to keep my treasures and heart on heavenly things and remind me I will not take any of these things with me. We purchased all new furniture, beds, couches, tables, chair, everything. I'm so thankful as I actually like my house and feel comfortable here.

Yes, I still think about having children and starting a family. I'm more open to sharing what we've been through, and the more I share, and as I write my story, I realize putting the words to the experience brings it out to light. The veil is lifted and being able to label and admit my hurt allows the past to sting a little less. I cry a lot less and laugh a lot more. I find humor in the smallest of situations and don't take things as seriously as I used to. Where there is no beauty, I know only God can find and will expose it. The last five years of my life have been a living nightmare; there are no cute words to describe it. However, I believe with my all that the only beauty to come out of all my losses will be produced by my Father in heaven; His amazing beauty will shine through and pierce through that darkness.

In the meantime, I will live joyfully and let God work. Thank You, Lord. I can't wait to meet my babies as I know they are in the best of care with You. I know You are working in me to make me the best heavenly mom I can be. Until that day, my prayer is that I will live the rest of my life here on earth to glorify You.

The End

Epilogue

A lot has happened since last May. It is now April 2014, and I am wondering what this year will bring.

In the past year, we celebrated our ten-year anniversary, sold our home in Maryland, purchased a new home in Delaware, I got a new job (which I'll be leaving), and Joe started his own business. Every single step was guided by God, and we are feeling His peace more and more each day. We also found a new church home, which we are grateful for. As a matter of fact, Joe was away on the men's retreat with our church when I first started the book. We have already forged strong friendships, and we look forward to growing more mature in Christ with our brothers and sisters.

Speaking of leaving my new job, yes, I have decided this is the best path for me. While we have been living in our new home the past several months, the last stitch of fretfulness left in my life has been my new job. It takes me back to when I was in the second grade, and I had to make a decision about the rest of my life. What will my family think? What will my friends thinks? You don't do this in society's standards. Then, I look to Jesus and immediately feel His loving gaze.

For the past five years, my body has expelled something from its womb around March or April of each year. This March or April, I will listen and act upon the urge I have been having the past couple of years to leave the mainstream. The Lord has forgiven, and forgotten, everything I have done since I was seven years old and first became saved. I'm going back to that time, to live my life the way I should have all along. I'm a giddy school girl again, feeling happier than on Christmas morning, and can't wait to see what the Lord has in store for the rest of my life—this time, with my white gloves on.

I have an inner peace and joy I have not felt in a very long time. It was a journey, one that affected my whole being physically, emotionally, spiritually, and mentally. God has worked His healing in me, and I am so thankful. If and when you embark on this journey to have God work within you, get ready for one heck of a ride. Our God is thorough; there is not one crevice of darkness in your heart and mind that will not be exposed. He brings light to the darkness, and He heals wholly, completely, lovingly, patiently, and into eternity. Thank You, Jesus.

Of course I still think it would be nice to start a family, but I think about it differently now. It does not control how I live my life nor do I think God is withholding it from me. Since we have moved closer to the beach, and closer to Christ, I am content with this new life. Joe and I straight up picked up and moved our lives from the last thirty-eight years in Maryland to the last few months in Delaware. When the Lord moves, it happens quickly, and His timing is perfect. As I reflect on the last five years, I am surprised by how much we have gone through, so much hurt and pain. Yet, what the Lord has brought about in us in the past six months has been divine healing.

The past is covered over with His love, and where His love is, no remnant of bitterness, anger or frustration remains. Jesus took all my shame to the cross and buried it. He left sin and death in the grave, conquered them, and flat out won, and arose on the third day with divine love. Only a Father in heaven who is absolute love can love and forgive someone like me. He will remember my sins no more and only see Jesus' perfect record when He sees me. I traded in my ashes, and in return, He gave me His beauty and then crowned me with forgiveness. I wear a crown that is everlasting and makes me an heiress with Christ in heaven. Thank You, Jesus.

I find divine humor in things and laugh a lot more. I don't take us and things so seriously, and I have more compassion for strangers. Thankfully, I was able to find my old journals as I could not remember if I had kept them or not. The nudge to write my book was stronger here, and I prayed to the Lord that if I were to write, I would need my journals. I looked in box after box, and being a bit disappointed, I offered up to God that I would do my best from my memory, which I knew was not reliable. One of my friends forwarded me the e-mails I had sent over the past couple of years, which was very helpful as well—thanks Kelly.

Then one routine day, wouldn't you know it, I find all my journals in a box. I thanked the Lord, but was also reticent about how I would react to opening up the floodgates again. Just when I thought I was over the past, here it is again for me to relive. Writing this has certainly been a journey through time and emotions. I cried and cried as I longed for the babies I lost. I missed my Rusty all over again and can't wait to play with him again. I consider what I've been through, and I lift it up to the Lord for Him to use. I don't know what will happen next, but I am confident in God's plans for me. My focus has shifted from making it (financially) in this world to sharing about the good news of the gospel. Will anyone listen? I don't know, but I know my God knows, and that is what matters most to me.

Since May 2013, we have not been pregnant and haven't been "trying" for a family either. Joe and I have been trying to put our lives back together and growing a stronger marriage through Christ. It's been a whirlwind of highs, lows, and confusion that we're learning, growing, and closing the chapter on. As we move on together, our prayer is that with each word that is read about our experiences, someone will repent, confess, start a personal relationship with Christ, be baptized, heal, and grow. I don't know if we'll ever have children on our own, but I am still hopeful, and I know that whatever comes our way, we will be held by heavenly arms that will never let us go.

As God has been healing me from the innermost this past year, one of the last tugs that was still bothering me was the unknown as to why I could not keep a pregnancy. I have been to many great doctors and have been pricked, prodded, probed, and diagnosed enough for a lifetime. I felt as if I had been kidnapped by aliens; like this is what they would do to human beings to figure out how our bodies function. There is a lot of speculation, but nothing is known for certain. I have never had a chromosomal test performed on the fertilized eggs; they were going to perform this test when we entertained the idea of IVF, but in the end we decided we would wait.

Today, I no longer ponder the unknown and think badly of myself. I am grateful that we have such a blessed life. God has completely turned us around and given us new lives to live. Joe and I say we lived the first part of our lives in a fidgety, restive way as we were living for ourselves, thanking God here and there for random things. Our prayer is that we will live the rest of our lives moving forward, living for the Lord, which produces love, joy, peace, patience, kindness, goodness, faithfulness, gentleness, and self-control (Galatians 5:22).

I have experienced immense physical pain, emotional pain, been lost and empty, and even near death. I have felt loved, abandoned, and depressed. I have lived life happy, or what I thought was happy, to feeling that nothing at all matters, not even my life. If there is one piece of advice I can offer, it is that you cannot fool yourself; you can try, but we all know deep down inside something is not right. We just choose to ignore it or numb it or suppress it. One thing that is absolutely certain is that you cannot fool God. Until you truly love the Lord your God with all your heart, all your soul, all your mind, and all your strength (Mark 12:30), I would argue with my dying breath that you cannot feel true contentment. I do not know how else one can find true inner peace and unexplainable joy for free.

Life is short compared to eternity. It is in our will and power to choose what to focus on. I've heard and read so many quotes and pick-me-ups, but I like both of the following a lot: "To be depressed, look to yourself, to be distracted, look to others, to be at peace, look to God." Amen and amen to that. This next one

I really like: "I am a nobody trying to tell anybody about the Somebody who can save everybody." Hallelujah! God wants us to enjoy our lives and bring others to the heavenly banquet table. I pray you look to our Father in heaven, through Jesus Christ, for incomparable joy and love.

So grateful and faithful when things are good,
So hateful and vengeful when things go bad,
So distasteful and wasteful bad can easily turn

So be mindful and kind-full to all,
So we may be graceful and peaceful, even if life seems unfair
That the Lord may be praised-full and pleased-full,
With the sweet aroma of our flare.

I look forward to the day when I wake up in heaven and see five beautiful children that resemble Joe and me. I want to hug every single one of them individually, and then I want all seven of us in a big family group hug, along with Rusty. Then all of us will be together as we worship our King as a family. Until that day, they are together as a family and in the best of hands. Joe and I will continue living in the now and enjoying every minute. Thank You, Jesus, for making all of this possible, in Your name, Amen.

About the Author

Su and her husband, Joe, live in Delaware, near the area beaches. Su's professional experience includes fifteen years in corporate business and management and has earned an MS degree in business. Joe and Su own and operate Spanners, an on-site service for computer and automotive repairs. Su enjoys hiking, traveling, writing and just hanging out with Joe.